DANCING WITH DECEPTION

CINDY HORNEMANN

Published by Cindy Hornemann
Peachtree City, Georgia 30269

Dancing With Deception

INTRODUCTION: THE FATHER WOUND

We have all come into this world helpless, dependent, and needing acceptance. We have a need to be treated as worthy and to be blessed.

What does a healthy father look like in the home? A righteous, godly father has an intimate relationship with God the Father. He exercises his spiritual leadership and covering in many ways. One of his priorities is to provide physical and emotional security. It is also to spend quality time with his children and make sure the home is filled with joy and safety. He sets an example of disciplining, training, and nurturing.

God is love, and the father's role of love is a vital one. When the father takes his healthy place in the home, it plays a significant role in the emotional development of a child's well-being. Children look to their fathers to lay down healthy rules and to enforce them.

A healthy father will wake up a child's spirit and help it grow into adulthood or womanhood. He calls them forward in life and helps lead them into their calling and destiny.

A father wound is a wound of the heart or soul that happens when the father is absent in some way and does not take the role or position he is called unto. The father wound can happen for many reasons. It can happen from the following:

1. Being Neglected: overlooked, undervalued, dismissed
2. Being Separated: divorce, sickness, death, war
3. Being Abused: mental, physical, sexual, spiritual
4. Being Controlled: oppressed, dominated
5. Being Denied: love, blessing, affirmation

These are just a few reasons for the father not taking his place in the home. Some fathers are in the home but unavailable or detached emotionally or spiritually. Many times, it is not the father's fault. We are in an imperfect world, and most of us come from some level of family dysfunction. Here are some negative results from a father wound:

1. Increased likelihood of low self-acceptance
2. Increased likelihood of dropping out of school
3. Increased likelihood of ending up in poverty
4. Increased likelihood of addiction to drugs and sex
5. Increased likelihood of having a child out of wedlock
6. Increased likelihood of deep emotional pain
7. Increased likelihood of performance orientation

This, however, is not always the case. Often, the result of an absentee father can create a wound that will impact the child's future in a negative way. It can interfere with that child's relationships into adulthood. When a person or child holds a concept of their father as angry, hot-tempered, uncaring, alcoholic, or critical, they tend to believe lies about themselves. For example:

1. I am unworthy.
2. I am stupid.
3. I am incompetent.
4. I am unlovable.

If we accept lies as truth, we may begin to experience depression and anxiety and may become angry. We may start performing to prove our worth through perfectionism and materialism—seeking addiction to cover the pain.

Christ has made us new, but the wounds inside our souls are not immediately addressed. It takes time and effort to walk with Jesus and to allow Him to heal our souls.

This book is about my journey of healing from my father wound and from many other life-controlling issues that tried to take my life. If Jesus can heal me, He can heal you. Nothing is too hard for Him. I am a perfect example of that. My purpose in writing this book is to bring hope and healing through the love of the Heavenly Father.

I was born in Texas during a tornado. My mom joked about it because my life has been somewhat of a tornado at times. Lots of negative and foolish activities whipped up storms that caused a lot of wind damage to my life.

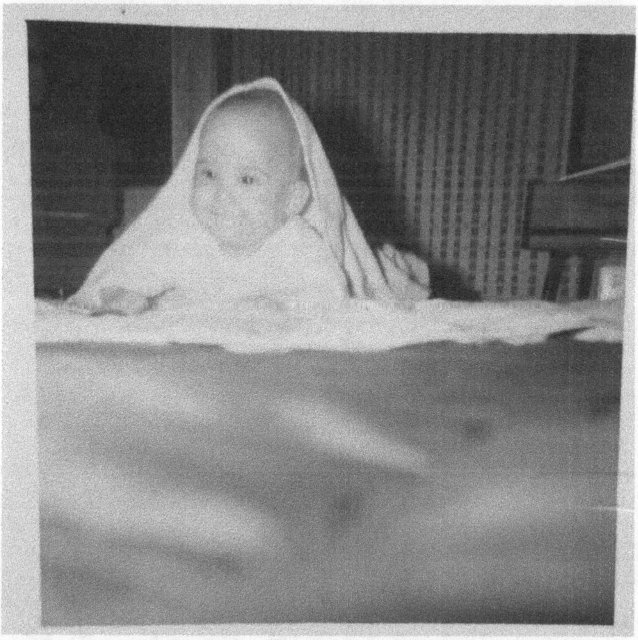

Cynthia; Germany; Five Months Old

The purpose of this book and sharing my journey is not to throw anyone under the bus or to expose anyone. It is to share my journey of mountain tops and valleys and to hopefully help people overcome similar battles.

My heart is to empower and give tools and strategies to fight against the enemy who wants to steal, kill, and destroy your life. My desire is that you draw close to an intimate relationship with Jesus Christ.

Twenty-seven years ago, I surrendered my life to Jesus Christ in the midst of one of those tornadoes. After many years of trying to do things my own way and in my own strength, I came to the end of myself and surrendered my life to doing God's will and not my own.

I desire to help people avoid the pitfalls that I stepped into. If you or your family have experienced any of the bad things I experienced, and you don't know there is complete healing in Jesus, I hope this book will help.

EARLY ORIGINS

I was born in Fort Hood, Texas. My father went into the army at an early age and met my mother on a blind date while they were in Kansas. My mother was a Kansas girl and had three sisters. They were all beautiful and had a great passion for fashion. All the sisters had their own flare and style. I admired my mother's sisters and was very close to them.

My maternal grandmother came from a family of sixteen brothers and sisters. My mother would often talk about the large family reunions they had. I remember going when I was a little girl.

One thing that stuck out to me was that my mom's family came from grandparents and great-grandparents who were strong in the Christian faith. My mother said her grandmother and grandfather were devoted Christians and wanted all their sixteen children to know the Lord and to be trained in the word of God.

I loved meeting with my aunts and mother and listening to stories about their youth. My mom shared with me that her aunts were powerful prayer warriors. She remembers going over to her Aunt Lela's house. They had their guitars out and were worshipping. They gave my mom and her cousin a blanket to play on while the aunties would worship and pray.

My mom said that one day, she told Aunt Lela that she did not feel well. Aunt Lela proceeded to pray strong warfare prayers over her in tongues. It scared my mom, and she said, "I didn't know that I was that sick." I thought that was a funny story.

Mom would also talk about going to the old tent meeting. She said that she and her cousins would stand up on top of their chairs so they could see the action. People were prayed for, and healing and miracles were happening.

Mom also shared how she was at her aunt's house, and a bad storm was coming. She watched as her aunts prayed against the storm, rebuked it, and commanded it to go away from the house in Jesus's name. Well, guess what? The storm went in the other direction. Isn't that great?

I am sharing these stories because I believe in generational blessings that can be passed down from generation to generation. However, one of my aunts had a struggle with alcoholism. Later in my life, this struggle, or curse, also hit me hard.

2

FATHER

Like all of us, my father was a wonderful man with many faults. He gave much of his life to serve our country and provide for our family. I want to say that I have forgiven my father and mother and all who have hurt me or brought pain to my life. This story will hopefully help and encourage you to forgive and let Jesus heal your past wounds.

My father was a Vermonter through and through. His family tree goes back years to Vermont. He was raised as an only child. His mother was very different than my mother's mom. Dad's mom was stoic and did not show much love. He was not raised with a Christian faith, but he was a great leader in the army. My dad had three uncles, and he was not raised around women or girls. However, he did love his mother very much.

After my parents' wedding, they waited three years to have my brother in Fort Benning, Georgia. Three years later, they had me in Fort Hood, Texas. When I was born, my dad was not allowed in the birth room. Things were a lot different back then.

Men had a different role. Most of all, they were expected to work hard and provide. They were to bring home a paycheck for the family.

Many were not prepared to care for the hearts of children and to nurture and teach them about the ways of God.

The lack of care for my heart from my father stemmed from different reasons. He was never around girls growing up. He was not raised with a lot of affection himself. It was also during a different time, and my father was a leader in the army and was trained to discipline men. This did not turn out well for me. I did not need a warrior or disciplinarian as a father. I needed love and nurturing and a father to care for my heart.

When I was six months old, we flew to Germany, where my father and our family were stationed for four years. Germany was all that I knew as a little girl. My mom told me that I had a maid who really loved me. She took me under her wing like her own child.

Four years later, my dad got an order to move back to the United States. We moved to Fort Campbell, Kentucky. I was a sensitive child. My mom said that the summer that we moved, I cried all summer. She was concerned and went to seek professional help for me. Counselors said that the problem was that I had been taken out of my security zone. I'd been taken away from my surroundings and everything I knew. Most of all, from the maid that loved me.

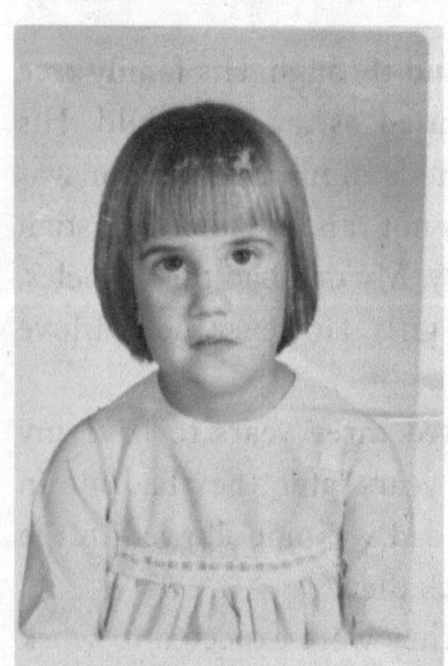

When I first started talking, the first words out of my mouth were, "I want coo-cook-kee and c-a-a-a-ndy." I was a stutterer. I am sure my father was thinking, "Oh, no," and wondering not only what to do with a sensitive little girl, but what to do with a stutterer.

Cindy at About Four Years Old

FEELING STUPID IN SCHOOL

I grew up with a chronic stutter. It was a handicap. I hated it. Especially being in an army family and subsequently often moving to new schools. It was traumatizing. I was smart and could read, but when it was my turn to read aloud in class, my heart would start beating fast, and I couldn't get a word out. Ugh! I felt stupid.

I discovered by changing schools so often that children can be brutal bullies. They said things and made fun of me without realizing they were leaving a lasting effect on my soul. You may have heard the childhood rhyme, "Sticks and stones may break my bones, but words will never hurt me." But this is one hundred percent false. Words not only hurt; they destroy.

The bullying I suffered may not have been as intense as others who I saw bullied, but I was a sensitive soul, and as I was growing up, I started to believe some of those lies. Later in my life, I realized these words had exercised negative power in my life. They were curses.

ATHLETE

I was an athlete most of my life. My mother put me in gymnastics and dance at a young age. I'm glad she did. I practiced hard and was good. I was extremely flexible and had a great rhythm.

STAGE

I remember that, at around six years old, I was a caterpillar in a dance recital; another year, I was a penguin. I recall having the black and white penguin outfit and even the beak. I was comfortable on stage, and I believe that was training for what was to come.

SIX YEARS OLD

My dad got orders to fight in the Korean War when I was six years old. It was a different time back then. This was before the era of cell phones, email, and social media. When a father went to war, there was no communication until they got back, except for letters.

While my father was away, we lived in an army apartment in Garden City, Kansas, where my mother was raised. Her parents lived there. I remember that time as wonderful memories. I am sure, however, that it was not always easy for my mother.

My mother, brother, and I were close. I remember taking my brother to school with my mom. I would spend the rest of the day with my mother. My mom would take me to the store and buy me a little candy on the way out. She was my security. I knew she loved me.

I remember a large field with no buildings across the street from our apartment. That's where I rode my new bike with its purple-sparkled banana seat. My brother would be with me on his bike. He was kind of a protector for me. I remember playing on that field with my brother and friends in the area. We used to see the most beautiful sunsets because of the flat terrain in Kansas.

My Christian grandparents lived there as well. I was able to spend time with them. I believe that, at that age, many good seeds of Christ's love were planted in me. When I went to my grandparents, they'd love on me and give me fun things to do, like arts and crafts. I still think of my grandparents on my mother's side very fondly. I believe a grandmother's prayers can go a long way. I am eternally grateful for this generational blessing.

FATHER

One warm day in Kansas, my brother and I were playing on the sidewalk. My father was coming home from the war, and there were lots of colorful balloons hanging around our home. I was young and didn't understand all that was going on, but I knew my mother was excited about something.

A car pulled up, and a tall, handsome man got out of the car. Mom went out to greet him. After hugging her, he came and hugged us. He bought my brother, mother, and me gifts from his journey. It was a celebration. My father had returned home after a year away in the army.

I remember my father taking my hands and swinging me up in the air and back down through his legs. Then, swinging me up even higher. I remember his feet were so big. I'd stand on the front of them and waltz. These are some of the positive memories I have of my father in those early years.

My father was an only child. His mother doted on him. I now suspect he wanted all my mom's attention. It was kind of a selfish thing. Even then, although I knew my mother was happy to have him home, everything had changed, and not necessarily for the good. I was longing for my mother and the close bond we had. That was all I knew. Now, it seemed that this tall man who was unfamiliar to my little heart was in the way.

I know he tried to do his best, but as a little girl, I sensed his lack of love and understanding of how to have a relationship with me. He was like a fish out of water when it came to raising me. I felt it, and it was painful.

As a little girl, I desperately wanted to please him and be good enough. I performed, danced, competed in sports, and excelled to get his attention. When I did well or won a game, I'd get his approval. But when I didn't do so well, I knew to get out of his way. *This is where I began to perform for approval.*

It was clear that he adored my mother. But at the time, I interpreted his desire for her as competition with us for her affection. I felt that us children were a burden. I don't think he meant for us to feel that way. He was only doing the best he knew.

I had a strong need to be approved of and loved by my father in an unconditional way. I longed to be his princess. There was a lot of pain and frustration in our relationship. As I became a teenager, it increased. I remember he would spank me with a wooden spoon if I had done something wrong. I am not against spanking, but it should be out of love and not out of anger.

I recall once, after he spanked me, I ran to my room screaming, "I hate you." That is something that has taken years to heal. I have heard the saying, "Rules without relationship equals rebellion." That seemed to be where I was headed.

When my mother saw Dad's temper flare up, she'd step in. Dad was the same with my brother. My mother finally told Dad he could not discipline me any longer and that she would do it. She was actively involved in our lives. She had a nurturing and loving heart. I believe this helped. She was the glue that stuck us together.

MOVED TO FORT LEAVENWORTH

We moved on post in Fort Leavenworth, Kansas, when I was around seven years old. Dad was an army officer, and this afforded many benefits. We had membership at the officers' club and swimming pool. Being raised as an army brat had its pros and cons.

We learned to be flexible and get along with new people and new surroundings. We were taught to respect our country and others. One of the cons was that being in a military family made establishing roots or lifelong friendships difficult.

DAD RETIRES

My dad finally retired after 20 years in the army. We bought a house off post in Fort Leavenworth, Kansas. I was there from the age of seven to twelve years old. These were good years. I had great friends in the neighborhood. We played kickball after school and kicked the can until dark. These are good memories of growing up with organic games and fellowship and not depending upon technology.

MOM IN ELEMENTARY YEARS

My mother was involved in my elementary school years. It seemed like she did everything. She was my Girl Scout leader. She took us to church. She volunteered as a Sunday school teacher. She was a teacher's aide. She helped my teacher set up holiday parties. I think her involvement in my life tremendously helped me in my later years.

INTRODUCTION TO JESUS

Cindy, age 12 1/2

My mother's sister, Aunt Pat, lived in Minnesota. Her daughter, Heidi, was my cousin. She was four or five years older than me. She loved Jesus, and I loved her. Neither of us had sisters. We visited one another a lot.

They had a boat on Lake Minnetonka. I remember being excited to visit. They would take us out on the boat. That is where I learned how to water ski. Heidi took me under her wings and loved me like a sister. I did not know until years later that I was so drawn to her because of the love of Jesus she had inside. I felt it and knew it was different.

When we were together for a week or so, and it was time to leave, I remember feeling strange. I was sad. Little did I know that many years later, she would be the one to open her home to me and help me recover.

At the age of twelve, Heidi gave me a Bible and asked me if I wanted to receive Jesus in my heart. I admired and loved her. This made it easy to believe what she said about God. I was very excited to receive Jesus and have a Bible. Once I received Christ, something inside of me felt warm and good.

GRANDMOTHER DIES

At the age of twelve, I came home from school one day and knew something was not right. I was sensitive to the atmosphere and people's emotions. My dad was crying, and there was a commotion in the kitchen between Dad and Mom. They told me that my dad's mother had just died. She was the stoic grandmother that I did not know well. My father, however, was very close to her, and it devastated him.

I had never seen my father cry. It was a strange feeling. My larger-than-life, very tall, very big military officer father showed weakness. In the army, he was trained for war. Showing weakness was not natural for him.

My father's parents still lived in Vermont. They had a nice piece of property and a nice house in the hills of the Green Mountain state. I believe his family lived in New England for many generations. My father went to help his father with his mother's funeral. When he returned, he told us his father was not well. His father invited us to go to Vermont to build on the original house and live there as his caregiver.

Dad said that my brother and I could finish school there in Vermont. Wow, this was a huge move. We had settled off post for four years and had bought a house. I had many good friends and neighbors, and I had been in gymnastics for years. It was time to move again. I did not want to leave my friends, but being raised around the military lifestyle, this was not unfamiliar.

MOVED TO VERMONT

The summer we moved to Vermont, I was twelve. My main goal was to get a friend and to find a gymnastics program. I remember being sad to leave my friends, but I recall running around on the seven acres of land in Vermont and being so free. It was beautiful.

We rented a house for a year while the house we were going to live in was being expanded. We built a suite for my grandfather to live in. We also built a full basement with another room and a four-car garage with a deck. It was stunning. It still is to this day.

CHURCH AND RELIGION

I attended grades seven through twelve in Vermont. My mom took us to an old Congregational church that had been in town forever. We went on holidays and sometimes on Sundays.

It was a pretty church with wooden pews, stained glass windows, and an organ. The service was formal and over my head. The preacher wore a robe. I wasn't used to this. I also didn't understand one word he said.

I know now it was religious, but it lacked relationship. The difference between religion and relationship with Jesus Christ is night and day. Religion has a form of godliness but denies its power. It is rules and performance-based and sets you up to fail every time. It's exhausting.

As I look back, I believe I had a call from God on my life. When my cousin gave me the Bible and I received Jesus, I moved to Vermont, and there was nowhere to grow. My mom tried to help me. She sent me to a weekend Christian camp with four of my friends.

This was a place where a lot of seeds of truth were planted in me. I felt that warm and peaceful feeling again. I did not really know about a personal relationship with Jesus, but the seeds of truth were being planted throughout my life.

When I was at camp, there was an alter call. The preacher called anyone up to the altar who wanted to give her life to Jesus. I stood there watching kids my age go to the altar and weep on their knees. I remember wondering what was happening. Why were they crying? The atmosphere was quiet and peaceful. I did not understand what was happening, but I knew it was good. Many years later, I was the one at the altar crying and repenting.

MOVING TO VERMONT AS A TEEN

Moving to Vermont in my teenage years was not easy. It was not a military community, and I believe new people did not frequently relocate there. I wanted to fit in. These made me vulnerable to influences. I remember I wanted to get into the right group. I found a gymnastics team and was one of the fastest girls in the school.

There was a boy named Jim who was blonde and cute. I wanted him to like me. His parents invited my parents to a party at their house, and I also went. There was Jim and a few other friends my age. I was in 7th grade.

There was a lake outside their house where the kids hung out. Jim suggested that we steal some beer from the parents. They had a huge cooler of beer on the deck. The party was going strong. It was getting dark. We stole the beer, and I drank it with Jim and the other kids so I would be accepted and liked.

I got dizzy and felt weird. I went to the boat and tripped and fell and cut my nose open. A flap of skin hung off my nose. Here I was, drunk at twelve from stolen beer, and blood was everywhere. I recall someone getting my parents. We went to the hospital for stitches. I remember being dizzy from the beer as the big operating spotlight was on me. I wondered if my parents knew I was drunk.

I wondered if I would have a scar on my nose forever. How embarrassing to walk around with stitches on my nose. Why did I need to fit in so badly? I believe I was looking for the love and acceptance that I wasn't getting from my father. I had a hole in my soul.

MEAN KIDS AS A TEENAGER!

Because I was new to the school, some of the kids were mean. The boys called me a flatlander and told me to go back to Kansas. I didn't even know what that meant. Some of the things said to me were that my nose was big and wide, that I had straight, stringy hair, and that I was a pirate's dream. This meant I had a sunken chest.

I was a stutterer. Some kids called me stupid because of this. I was, however, fun and full of life and had a lot of friends. I was a great athlete and made lifelong friends in dance, gymnastics, field hockey, track, and the swim team. I wasn't just an average team member. Sometimes, we'd win state championships and even establish new records.

The question I had was, If I was so popular and starting to fit in, why did these words spoken about me go into my heart this deeply? It was because I did not know who I was. I was trying to find my identity and was overly sensitive.

The word curses spoken about me took root. I believed the lies. Later down the road, they propelled me in the wrong direction.

JUNIOR HIGH SCHOOL YEARS

Looking back on my life, I believe I was marked and called by God. Maybe it was when I said "Yes" to the Lord with my cousin that God heard that prayer. However, the devil heard it, too, and there was a battle over my life.

The Bible says, "My people perish for lack of knowledge" (Hosea 4:6). I also see that the hand of God protected me as I went through volatile situations. I know now that people can open the door to good or evil in their lives. In addiction recovery programs, they call these gateways.

These are curses that can come to us from previous generations. They give us a strong propensity toward certain sins and bondages. Most curses will pass from generation to generation until they are broken.

Jesus paid the price for our freedom. Satan is defeated, but we must not be ignorant of His schemes. Satan will not give up one inch of ground until we force him to! We must know we have victory. We must then stand in faith until we EXPERIENCE THE VICTORY. When we stand in the name and authority of Jesus, Satan has no choice but to flee:

1. Matthew 11:12: "And from the days of John the Baptist until now, the kingdom of heaven suffers violence, and the violent take it by force."
2. James 4:7: "Therefore submit to God. Resist the devil and he will flee from you."
3. 2 Corinthian 2:14: "Now thanks be to God who always leads us in triumph in Christ and through us diffuses the fragrance of His knowledge in every place."

God has given us the keys to the kingdom of heaven, but He does not force us to use them. When Israel entered the land of Canaan, God said, "I have given you the land." But they had to go in, possess it, and evict the inhabitants who were there. This is a picture of how we possess the land of our body, soul, and spirit.

Going back to my junior high school days, I now see the gateways I had opened, not knowing I would become addicted or that it may be the beginning of dangerously bad habits.

I finally found my friend group in the seventh grade in Vermont. I had a great group of friends, and we still stay in touch. I wondered why some of my friends did not have to go through the things I had to go through. Everyone is unique, and their destiny, gifting, and generational bent are different.

We all have a different road or path to take. I had alcohol addictions and other things in my family tree. Some people can drink in high school and college, stop drinking, and have a perfectly normal life. Others can take a drink of alcohol and cannot stop. I think my addictions grew a little over time.

I excelled in gymnastics, field hockey, track, and swim team. My gymnastic years were from the age of six to fifteen. I played field hockey from junior high through college. I started swimming at the age of twelve and competed until I was eighteen.

All these years of working with a team imparted to me discipline and focus. I learned to win and lose in a healthy way and to be a team player. It was a great training ground for the ministry God was calling me into in the future. I did not know it, but He was preparing me, and God does not waste anything.

I recently went home to Vermont to visit my mother. She asked me to help declutter and empty out a chest full of old stuff. It was no accident that it was all my trophies and jackets and award ribbons from my high school years.

SWIMMING

As I sorted through my memorabilia, I recalled that one of the biggest successes of my athletic career was swimming. I started at the age of twelve on the Springfield swim team and learned quickly. We practiced two times a day during the summer. We were an unstoppable team with a great coach.

The swim team was the place to be. We were a unit and had fierce determination and support for one another. Over the years, I was awarded for being the most improved swimmer. Then, my growth excelled even more.

One summer, I took advanced lifesaving to become a lifeguard. I also went to a University of Maine swim summer camp to prepare for the swim season. I will never forget how hard that camp was. But it got me into the best shape of my life. I believe that was part of my success that year on the swim team.

I was a lifeguard and was on the swim team for many years. When I was sixteen or seventeen, our team was in the state competition. I was on a relay with one of the girls who was breaking records. We won the girls' relay and broke the record for the state, not just once, but many times. We were unbeatable and proud of it!

PAGEANT, PARTYING, SENIOR YEAR

I excelled in my senior year in another way. I participated in the Miss Junior Miss Pageant and won second runner-up. I did a jazz dance for the talent portion of the contest. I received a big trophy for Miss Poise and Appearance and a hundred-dollar award. I did well because of the years of gymnastics, dance, and being on stage.

My picture was in the newspaper the next day. I rode in the Miss Junior Miss convertible at the Springfield alumni annual parade with Miss Junior Miss and the first runner-up. Some people would have been uncomfortable doing this. I wasn't because I was in my element.

As a reward for becoming second runner-up, my parents took me on a trip with them to New York City during the Christmas holiday season.

OLD STUFF NOT LOOKED AT YET

As I looked through the memories, trophies, and things my mother had saved, it was a good reminder of how God was with me and training me. These positive experiences in my life shaped me and my confidence. Looking back, there were other things shaping me that were not so positive.

Growing up in that area of New England, there was not a lot to do. There was a movie theater and a bowling alley. The environment did not have a big Christian community. A few of my friends went to a Catholic church because their parents made them. They were always complaining about it.

My family were alcohol drinkers, and so were my friends. We drank a lot. My friends and I would get together on weekends to hang out and party. Someone would find a place in a big field or on someone's property in the middle of nowhere and set up a bonfire. Then, we would pull a truck around, open the tailgate, and set up a keg of beer. Word would get out where the party was. We would get around the fire and drink and socialize and get drunk.

PROMS AND COTILLION, SCHOOL PLAY

Even though I was insecure in some areas and was a stutterer, I was outgoing and full of life and loved people. During my senior year, I was in my town's annual Apple Blossom Cotillion. Couples dressed up in formal attire and performed dances together as a group.

On an evening when the whole town was invited to watch us perform, judges selected the Cotillion queen and her court, which consisted of three couples. I was not chosen to be the queen, but I did get into the court.

Cindy Wins "Poise and Appearance" Competition

During my senior year, I was also in the school play. The play was *Bye, Bye Birdie*. I never tried out for a speaking part because of my stuttering. But I was happy to be one of the 1950s girls in the play who was cheering on the singer in a concert. We got to wear our 1950s poodle skirts and black and white patent leather shoes. There were a lot of us. It was fun to be in that production.

Ms Junior Miss Second Runner-Up; Alumni Parade in Springfield, Vermont

IN ALL MY HIGH SCHOOL YEARS, I WENT TO FIVE PROMS. ONE PROM memory that sticks out is my junior year prom. I don't think I wanted to be with the guy I was with. I was upset. I believe I wanted to be with the guy my friend was with. Anyway, I remember going to an after-hours party after the prom.

There were a lot of experienced partiers there. They had some hard alcohol that they offered to me. I drank some and blacked out. My brother showed up at the party and ended up carrying me home over his shoulder in my prom dress.

Cindy's 1981 Senior High School Photo

Blacking out at such an early age is not a good sign. I did not know I was in trouble. I did not know I had a problem with addiction and that, down the line, it was going to try to take my life and destiny. One thing I did know was that I had a severe headache the next day, which was not fun. That was the beginning of many hangovers.

PARTYING WITH THE COACH AND TOP ATHLETE

The girl we all looked up to was a fabulous swimmer. She chose our team to swim on. We were overjoyed. She had a pool at her house. One day, she invited the lifeguards and swim team leaders to her home to hang out and swim.

We were having a good time when she took us up to her room and brought out a bunch of marijuana. I mean a lot. Come to find out, I heard her parents sold marijuana!

It was strange to see a fellow swimmer who I looked up to getting high and smoking weed and offering it to us. My friends, who were also leaders on the swim team, enjoyed it. I never really enjoyed pot. It made me paranoid.

High School Graduation - 1981

One night, after getting high, I went to the grocery store with my friends. I remember walking in, and it seemed as if the whole store stopped and stared at me. Ugh! Pot was not fun for me! I knew a lot of high-strung people who loved it. It helped them calm down.

Our coach also invited us to a party at his house. I looked up to him, as well. He also brought out the alcohol and pot. What was happening? Coaches and athletes in authority and influence should be people of integrity. They are responsible for covering those under their care and being good examples.

The definition of responsibility is the role of obligation to control personal behavior and moral obligation. This was an example of leadership being twisted and no moral standard. I looked up to these people and began to think this was normal. I was being desensitized. Next was sex. It was a deadly combination.

8

SEX BEFORE MARRIAGE

As I got older, a few of my friends in my group had steady boyfriends. Some of them had sex. I was so busy with my friends, sports, and other activities that I had never really thought about it much.

I think it was junior year that I dated a few guys. One wanted me to sleep with him. I was not interested. Another guy in my senior year made a move on me after the prom. He was tall, dark, and handsome, and a top athlete. He was popular and fun to be around. That night after the prom, we were at a park. I felt something in his pocket. It was a condom. What? I was kind of insulted. Now I knew what he was after, and that was a real turn-off for me. Our relationship faded after that.

God designed sex, and the Bible honors marriage. When two unmarried people engage in sexual intercourse, they are defiling God's good gift of sex. They have now entered a soul tie with each other. There will be many problems. Love is passionate and a wonderful thing. God gives sexuality to married couples as a type of cement. A bond that helps hold hearts together.

However, many fall into the trap of counterfeiting and give in to a sexual relationship before marriage. This is what happened to me at eighteen. Sex before marriage is a door that does not need to be opened until the right time. I experienced this and the great amount of damage it did to my life.

I had a boyfriend the summer after my senior year. We will call him Sam. He was a few years older than me. I had known him and his family for years. He was handsome, funny, and a great athlete. We got closer to each other during the summers.

He was a top-notch swimmer and a lifeguard. He was in my group that worked at the pool. We worked hard and partied hard. Many parties were at his house. He began to pay attention to me at these parties. We found ways to make out or kiss behind a door or some-where away from people. We worked together, played together, and partied together.

I was falling for him. I could not stop thinking about him. Every girl would've loved to have been his girlfriend. He was kind of a man's man and loved his friends, too. The summer that I was eighteen was the summer I believe I fell in love with him. I am not sure if that is what it was, but it sure felt like it.

One weekend, our coach and his wife were going out of town. They asked Sam to house-sit. He invited me over, and there we were, all by ourselves. This was the night that changed many things. I gave my heart, soul, and body to him that night. It was a mistake that would take years to recover from.

I am an all-or-nothing type of person. I love and feel deeply. I feel like I have an extreme call of God on my life. So, for years, I went extremely in the opposite direction. I was tossed back and forth by deception and lies I believed about myself and others. I never would have believed that opening this door to sex before marriage would lead me into the horrors of the sex industry years later.

The negative results of sex outside of marriage are many. This includes a high number of sexually transmitted diseases, many more abortions, and many children born without both parents. Couples who have sex before marriage have twice the rate of divorce of those who wait until marriage. Plus, there are negative emotional long-term consequences.

Unfortunately, it is normalized to have sex before marriage. It seems this day, if you take a biblical stand on the issue, you are called Old School or worse. Call me old school. I have personally experienced the pain and trauma of opening the sex-before-marriage door. It almost killed me.

God gave us His Word and His Holy Spirit to guide us in this world. He does not want it to rain on our parade. He's not a party pooper. He's our Creator and loves us and knows us. He knows what will open the door to trauma and problems.

If you have had sex before marriage and have never given your life to God, God's mercy is available to you through repentance and believing in Christ for salvation. The same is true if you are a disciple of Christ who has fallen into sexual sin. He will restore you if you repent.

So, practically speaking, how can you succeed at waiting so you can gain a lifetime of sexual fulfillment?

1. Decide your boundaries ahead of time.
2. Date in public places. You are more likely to maintain your boundaries in a crowded restaurant than in an apartment watching a movie.
3. Stay active. Exercise, work on projects, or help others.
4. Share a purpose. Couples in service, ministry, or volunteer work have a reason bigger than themselves to stay pure. Be a role model.

God wants you to be holy. So, you should keep clear of all sexual sin (1 Thessalonians 4:1-5).

Wow! If I knew back then what I know now! I did not have this understanding back then and experienced some hard consequences.

However, I have moved forward and have received much healing. Now, I hope I can help people learn from my pitfalls. My pain and mess brought me to my knees. It drew me to Jesus. So, for that, I am grateful. I now use my mess as a message. Hopefully, it can impact someone's life by sharing.

9

HEADED TO COLLEGE

In some of my high school classes, it was as though I wore foggy goggles. I could not see clearly or understand the subjects. It was mainly math and chemistry. I had an older math teacher in 7th grade whose age had apparently caught up with him. He was quite forgetful and would get off track.

I didn't learn much. I got behind, and it was difficult to catch up. I believe now that not all children thrive in the school system. Everyone learns differently and has different gifts and talents.

It seems that now there is more help for those who don't fit into the mold of the public school system. When I gave my life to the Lord and went to massage school, I had to take anatomy and physiology courses. They were hard classes, but what was different was that I had given my life and studies to the Lord. He was helping me. I was in my lane of calling and aligned with what God wanted me to do. It was amazing. I got all straight As. It was not easy, but it was as if the foggy goggles had been taken off.

18-Year-Old Cindy at Lake Champlain in Burlington, Vermont

My grades and test scores were not good enough to get into a good college. At the end of my senior year, my friends talked about what colleges had accepted them. There was excitement in the air. I was not too excited about it for myself but for them.

I didn't know where I was going or what I would do. It was a strange feeling because all my friends from seventh grade up and I had lived life together. Now, we were about to go our separate ways.

I had a good friend named Suzy from a neighboring school who I met at field hockey camp. We hit it off and spent a lot of time together. She told me that she had applied to Lake Champlain College. It was a small private school in Burlington, Vermont. That was the big college town. It had three large colleges and other small ones.

There were a variety of majors at Champlain. It had fashion, secretarial, accounting, and many others. I had taken a lot of secretarial classes in high school because I loved the teacher. I did a lot of typing and three years of shorthand. This was just as computers were coming out.

I decided to apply to Champlain after getting encouragement from Suzy. To my amazement, I was accepted. Suzy was excited. We both were. She asked if we could be roommates together. Her request was approved. That was the beginning of our relationship. It continued after college.

SAYING GOODBYE TO MY BOYFRIEND

I shared earlier how I gave my heart and body to my boyfriend the summer before college. All I could think about was him. I gave myself fully and was deeply in love. Now, it was time to go to college. My boyfriend was going to college as well but in another state. It was weird. So many changes. We decided to stay in touch and save ourselves for each other until after college.

Champlain was about two hours from my home. When my parents brought me to college, I was excited about something new and to be free. As I look back now, I realize that I was not in good mental or spiritual shape and was not prepared for what the world and college had to offer.

I went to college to get an associate degree in executive secretarial science. What I should have gotten was a degree in Party 101 and Party 201! I really appreciate my parents paying for my college. I know they really cared. I do not know how I graduated because it was all kind of a blur. I stayed in an all-girls house, a type of dorm.

There were about 30 girls living in the house. I enjoyed it and built great relationships. I always had someone to laugh or cry with. I was social, and that was a great benefit. I have great memories of the girls.

The condition of my heart and soul was not good when I went to college. The party atmosphere in college reinforced my addictions and hid my pain. My heart was in pain from my father's rejection of me and his lack of love. I had opened the door to alcohol, drugs, and sex. I think at this point, I might have been a full-blown alcoholic, or at least quickly on my way.

The town of Burlington had every kind of bar and club and was active every night with having so many colleges in one area. My friends in my dorm always wanted to go out. We would put on makeup and nice clothes, hit the bars and clubs, and drink and dance.

One of my friends had a car, and she was an experienced partier, even more than me. She was from a big city and was at the school for fashion. She had nice makeup and nice clothes. She took me on as her party buddy. She taught me about makeup, clothes, boys, and things I probably did not need to know. We would go out and get really drunk and dance all night. I remember having an 8:00 a.m. math class and showing up hung over. I don't know how I graduated, but I did.

One thing that helped me a lot in college is that I was on the field hockey team. That was a great way to keep in shape and out of trouble. In my second year of school, my best friend from high school got accepted to Champlain and joined me. She and I had been playing field hockey together since seventh grade. Now we were together again, and playing field hockey! It was a great experience. We got to travel with the team. We won a lot and lost a lot. It didn't matter. We were together.

I remember the end of the school year when my boyfriend and my best friend's boyfriend came to visit us at school. They had a van and got us tickets to the Doobie Brothers concert that was playing in Saratoga Springs, New York. It was a great trip and a great concert. We drank a lot and got drunk a lot. But that wasn't anything new. I did sense my boyfriend was not quite so drawn to me as I was to him. I am not sure he gave me his heart. However, he liked me a lot, and we had fun spending time together.

My boyfriend liked his parties, his friends, and his sports. He also liked his freedom. I think at this point, there were signs that this relationship was not a two-way street. Looking back now, I'm not sure if maybe he did not know how to open his heart to a woman. Or if God was protecting me. I think it was both.

In my second year of college, some friends and I went on a four-hour road trip to see my boyfriend. His sister was there as well. We were going to stay with her. Four of us went. We partied the whole way. When I got there, it was as if a freight train hit me.

My boyfriend's sister told me that he (the one I gave my heart, soul, and body to) had found a girlfriend at college. I went numb. Something shot into my heart. Betrayal, abandonment, grief, loss, pain. All of the above. My heart was shattered. I did not know how to deal with this kind of pain. It's amazing how we can remember these moments. This was a pivotal moment in my life. It changed me.

I shut down my heart and put walls around it. I was determined never to be hurt again. I did not have coping skills for this type and level of pain. All I knew was to party more, have fun, and bury the pain. I felt a deep sense of rejection. I was alone and inadequate.

I have learned that sometimes things are a protection from God, which at the time may feel like rejection. *So, party hard or party until you puke because, tomorrow, you may die.* This was the motto. This had been a motto for a long time in my life. No wonder I was going down the wrong path—a path of deception and destruction.

Graduation from Champlain College 1983

I did manage to graduate from college with an associate degree. It had to have been a miracle that I graduated. I had a low-grade point average, but I got my diploma, which helped me get jobs.

The summer after graduation, four of my friends from college decided to stay in Burlington to get a summer job and rent a house together. This was a fun summer. I got a job at a steakhouse. My roommates got jobs at restaurants or clothing stores. I remember the feeling of being free and on my own and grown up. We were beginning to fly.

10

STOWE

I got a call from my old college roommate, Suzy. She had an offer to open and manage a new clothing store in Stowe, Vermont. She asked if I was available to help her. I was. She had a cute apartment at the bottom of the mountain and asked if I wanted to share it with her. Of course, I wanted to share it!

Stowe, Vermont, is known for its trails and ski slopes. Its beauty is breathtaking in every season. I was beyond excited. This was right before the snow season started. She said that after I helped her open the store, I could stay in the apartment, but I would have to look for another job. Stowe had many resorts, restaurants, and places to work during the ski season. Having my college degree helped me get a job.

When I finished helping my friend open the store, I went up and down the mountain, putting in my application for the winter. I finally got a job at a 5-star resort named "Top Notch at Stowe." As a waitress, the goal was to work evenings. That was the money-maker. The place was beautiful. It had chandeliers in the dining room, high-class décor, and lots of floor-to-ceiling windows with breathtaking views.

They had a lot of tennis tournaments in the summer and ski events in the winter. The Sunday brunch was full of the best food and ice sculptures that were handcrafted right there on site. I had never seen anyone make an ice sculpture. It was impressive. The place drew a lot of famous people, as well.

To reach my goal of working the evening shift, I had to start at breakfast and then graduate to train for the lunch shift. I had to be there at 5:00 a.m. to prepare breakfast. I was not alone. I was being trained with two other girls, Lori and Michelle.

Lori and Michelle were drifters. They loved to travel and experience beautiful places. They were my age. They were in Stowe for at least a year. They were potheads and hippies. Even though I was not a pothead, we got along well.

No one had a car. I remember one day during a snowstorm, I had to hitchhike to the restaurant. Lori and Michelle were there right with me. I cannot imagine hitchhiking today. We finally graduated from the breakfast shift and were now promoted to lunch.

One story that jumps out to me is when I hitchhiked to a Grateful Dead concert. Lori and Michelle told me the concert was in Rhode Island. They wanted me to come. Well, it sounded like an interesting experience. I remember hitchhiking with them to Rhode Island. We got a ride with others who were going to the concert. There was a lot of drinking and partying on the way. We arrived at the concert drunk.

When we arrived, I remember thinking how wild it was. There were vendors selling all kinds of tie-dye things. Folks were dancing wildly and high on acid and who knows what else. Drugs and alcohol were everywhere. The drug-induced mantra was love, joy, and peace.

As I look back now, I know it was counterfeit love, joy, and peace. It brought me back to the thought of Woodstock. The famous music festival was held in New York in 1969. I can only imagine what that was like. I did not even like this kind of music. I loved R&B, Motown, and pop music. This was far from that!

But I was young and wanted to experience life. I am not sure how we made it home from that concert. I am Grateful Alive! Happy to be alive and thanking God that he covered me even in my ignorance.

We survived the Grateful Dead and returned home to Stowe. In a short period, Michelle, Lori, and I graduated from lunch shift to dinner.

My roommate moved out. I had the apartment to myself. The group of people I worked with at Top Notch became a type of family. We spent a lot of time together and built relationships. A few of my friends from Top Notch moved in with me, and that became the place to be. We hung out, rode bikes, skied, played hacky sacks, and listened to music.

During the dinner shift, Lori, Michelle, and I worked in the beautiful dining room. We had to wear nice outfits to serve. We wore long sleeves, white ruffled blouses, a long brown skirt, and nice shoes. It was a classy place.

I was extremely nervous about my first table. It was a table of guys about 30 years old who were there on a skiing trip. I introduced myself and began to tell them the specials. One of the specials was a pound-and-a-half lobster, which was popular. I was relieved they were all nice and relaxed. I was also relieved they all ordered the same thing. They ordered the special pound-and-a-half lobster. This should be easy.

I put the order in, and a little while later, I served them all the lobster. They looked happy. I went back to the kitchen to give them some time to enjoy their meal. When I went back out, they requested crackers. I was wondering why they would want saltines. I went back and placed saltine crackers on round plates and gave them to each person. To my shock, they started laughing hysterically. They couldn't stop.

I did not know why they were laughing. But it was so funny to watch them, I joined in. When they calmed down and could finally talk, they told me they wanted the "lobster crackers," not saltines. They got a good laugh, and I didn't mind. I am easygoing. They gave me a great tip.

I saw them later that night at the local bar and dance club. They said, "There's the cracker lady." They bought me a drink and cheers'ed me for giving them a good laugh and making their night special!

The group of us at Top Notch got closer. My friends Lona and Bradley worked in the kitchen. They were young and in love with one another. Bradley asked Lona to marry him. She had just bought a new

Volkswagen hatchback and had never been anywhere outside of Stowe.

She didn't want to marry right away. She told me she had never traveled and wanted to travel for a year. Then she'd come back and see if she still wanted to marry him.

She asked me if I would travel with her across the country. We could end up in California and spend a year either in San Diego at the beach or in the Lake Tahoe area in the mountains. I talked to my parents and decided it would be a good adventure.

I put some money aside in preparation for the trip. We had some personal belongings, a tent, and our mountain bikes. Today, two girls staying in tents as they cross the country is not safe, but back then, it was fine.

11

CROSS COUNTRY TO TAHOE!!!!

Lona and I quit our job and let my roommate take over the apartment in Stowe. We packed everything and started on our new adventure. It took us approximately twelve days to get there. We started in Vermont and went to Canada to visit friends. We went to Michigan and Minnesota. Then, we visited Mount Rushmore in South Dakota. After that, we went to Colorado and then Utah.

While in Minnesota, we stayed at my aunt and uncle's house. My aunt was my mother's sister. My cousin lived there, too. It was the early 80s, and the singer and musician Prince was popular in Minnesota. He had just finished the Purple Rain movie. His hangout was the First Avenue nightclub, where part of the movie was filmed.

My cousin got Lona and me tickets to see the Godfather of Soul himself, James Brown, at the First Avenue club. There was a big crowd at the door. My cousin said it was Prince who was coming to see James Brown. Wow. Both Prince and James Brown were trailblazers in R&B and funk music. Even though they were not my style of artists, it was a fun experience.

Lona and I kept pressing on toward our destination. We ended up in Tahoe City, California. It was right before snow and ski season. The beauty was breathtaking. The smell of fresh air and pine trees was crisp and inviting. The beauty of the lake and the mountains surrounding it was something I had never seen before. Lona really loved it because she was a mountain and ski person. I was more of a beach person but was open to staying in Tahoe.

We pitched a tent and slept at a campsite in Tahoe City, where we got to know the area. We knew there were several ski resorts around Lake Tahoe. There was a grocery store nearby, and we thought we would see if there were any Vermont license plates in the parking lot. We found one and waited for the person to come out of the store.

The person who owned the car was a guy our age with red hair and freckles. We approached him. He said his name was David, and he was from a place in north Vermont, and that he owned a ski shop in the Squaw Valley ski resort. He rented a house in Squaw Valley and happened to have a room with two beds in it for rent. Wow, this was an amazing breakthrough. I can now see that God guided me even when I did not know it!

Squaw Valley ski resort is located on the North Shore of Lake Tahoe. It is one of the largest ski areas in the United States. It was home to the 1960 Winter Olympics. We decided to choose Squaw Valley and take the room in David's house. We planned to get jobs on the mountain at Squaw Valley. Employees were given free ski passes. What we needed now was snow. We had to wait about a month until the mountain opened.

While Lona and I and all of Tahoe waited for ski season to open, we got to tour Tahoe and do some sightseeing. We did not have much money, so we survived on Ramen noodles and cheap wine. While we waited, we applied at Squaw Mountain for different jobs. I applied for and got a job at a restaurant named High Camp on the top of the mountain.

I had to take the tram every day. The elevation of the base of Squaw Valley was 6,200 feet above sea level. The top at High Camp, where I worked, was 9,050 feet. It took some time to get acclimated. The view was spectacular.

While waiting for the mountain to open, Lona and I decided to drive to Lake Tahoe and walk on the beach and rocks. It was a beautiful day. As we walked, we saw two guys coming our way. They were also out enjoying the day and the lake and looked to be about our age.

We ran into them and began to have a conversation. We hit it off immediately. They were also from New England and were brothers. They were handsome and in good shape. I came to find out that they were both on the US ski team and in Tahoe for training.

The brothers asked us out to dinner. We had a great time. I started dating the older brother, Chase, and Lona dated the younger brother, Brian. We spent a lot of time with them. They trained in the gym while waiting for ski season.

The snow season finally started. Lona got a job as a ski patrol, and I started working at the High Camp restaurant. Part of the duties were to bring food supplies up on the tram and to clean and open the restaurant for the upcoming season.

I worked with great people. The bartender's name was Susan. She was a lot of fun. She made going to work a joy. When it was time to close and clean up, she would give all the waitresses free shots. We would come down the tram very intoxicated, singing and laughing. We would usually take the last tram down alone at the end of the day. We had a good time.

Squaw Valley was beautiful. It's in California. Famous people were often seen skiing there. If there were someone famous on the mountain, the employees would use their walkie-talkies to notify everyone. One day, while I was working, I heard Huey Lewis and the News (the 80's band) were on the ski tram heading to High Camp. Remember that this was the 80s, and they were one of the most popular soft rock bands at that time. They were well-known for the theme song for the *Back to the Future* movie.

To my surprise, they sat at my table. I was star-struck and shaking. They wore ski outfits and hats, but I knew it was them. I could tell because Huey had a very strong dimple on his chin, which was very noticeable and attractive. I had on my cool new pair of sneakers with wings on the sides. I always liked to be different.

I was nervous as I served them. They ordered one round of Bloody Mary's for the table. The whole band was there. I asked Huey if I could see his ID. I was testing him to see how he would react. He laughed and said, "No." Then I said, "Then can I have your autograph?" He gave me his autograph with a smile. He was a very kind man.

After drinking the first round, they called me back to the table. Huey asked what my name was and told me they liked my shoes. He said they were putting on a concert in Reno on Saturday. He made me an offer. He said if I got them another round of drinks, he would give me two free tickets to the show. Wow, what a great offer! I got the drinks for them, and he asked me my name. He got out a piece of paper and wrote it down.

He instructed me that when I went to the concert in Reno, I should go to the second ticket booth for family and friends. He told me that when I got there, I needed to say my name and ask for the tickets. He said there would be tickets for me and a guest. He also said that we could go backstage to the party afterward. Unbelievable! What a fabulous day!

Huey then proceeded to put the paper with my name on it in the front zipper pocket of his ski outfit. Oh no! He had been drinking at a high elevation, which made people drunker faster. I was afraid that he would not remember putting my name in his ski jacket. I was still going to give it a shot.

Who was I going to take to the concert? After Huey and his band skied off, all of us employees were excited. I decided to invite my bartender friend, Susan. We could not wait. We would take her car. It was a cute VW bug. We got all dressed up on Saturday for the concert in Reno. I didn't want to get our hopes up that the tickets were there. So, we decided we would go out on the town in Reno if we didn't get into the concert.

When we arrived, the concert was packed. It was hard to find a parking spot. We went up to the family ticket booth. I gave my name and asked for two tickets. Sure enough, there they were. Susan and I had tickets to the best seats at the concert. We had such a great time. The party afterward was special. It was family-friendly. They had soda and food. The band all sat around the table, greeted us, and signed our autographs. What a great memory.

We returned to Lake Tahoe after the concert. Lona and I continued to date the brothers on the US ski team. They spent a lot of time at our house. I was sexually active, but I was still protecting my heart from past betrayals. I was just having fun. Yet I knew something was not right with my relationship with Chase. We fought a lot. I just couldn't put my finger on why.

When ski season ended, Lona returned to Stowe to get married. Chase stayed to get an apartment in Squaw Valley. I decided to stay and move in with him. Making it to the US ski team is not easy. Chase's father trained him and his brothers from an early age. I think he had them on snow skis at the age of three.

Chase had a dream of being on the US ski team. He put all his eggs in that one basket and went for it. On one of Chase's important races in Switzerland, there was a whiteout. This means the weather prevents you from seeing the contours of the ground and other identifying markers. It makes it difficult to navigate safely.

He landed in the wrong place and twisted his knee. He tore it and all the ligaments. He had to come home to Tahoe, where expert surgeons worked on many athletes, especially skiers in the area.

12

BEGINNING OF BODYBUILDING

Chase's career on the US ski team was over. He was a gifted skier and had skied all his life. He was offered a job as a coach after his knee healed. It was a good fit for him. After his operation, he had to spend a lot of time in the gym rehabilitating his knee.

I had always been in sports and was an athlete, but in Tahoe, I was not doing any sports. I wanted to spend time with Chase. He invited me to the gym while he rehabilitated his knee. He taught me how to work out. My body responded quickly. It started to change shape and get stronger. People noticed and asked me if I was working out.

I got attention from the way I looked. It was such a deception because I believed the lie that I was not smart or pretty. Also, the lack of attention from my father left me with a need for outside validation. I did not know that I was already perfect and beautiful in the sight of my heavenly Father. I had felt the rejection of people and close men in my life. Now, people were noticing me and giving me attention for the way I looked. I was hooked!

At the same time, Chase's knee was healing, and he was training me hard in the gym. I had great genetics. My body was easy to sculpt. The changes came quickly. Chase heard that a Lake Tahoe bodybuilding competition was coming up soon. He wanted to sign me up.

It was the first bodybuilding show in the area. I was excited and ready to train hard.

Chase only had a little time to train me for this show. We worked diligently and with great focus. I was becoming a "gym rat." A gym rat is someone who spends a lot of time exercising in the gym. It could describe someone who is obsessed with the condition of her body.

When ski season finished, Chase moved out of Squaw Valley and into an apartment in Tahoe City. I moved in with him. It was convenient because it was very close to the gym. The gym was named Iron Works. A sweet couple owned it and had three children. I spent many hours at the gym, and we became like a family.

Because I have an all-or-nothing personality, I decided to put everything into this Tahoe bodybuilding show. The gym had a lot of free weights and exercise equipment and an aerobic studio. They also sold vitamins and health products.

I used the aerobics studio with mirrors to work on my bodybuilding routine. When bodybuilders do their individual routines, they can choose their own music. The routine consists of doing poses and dance moves to show judges their symmetry, muscularity, conditioning, posing, and stage presentation.

The owners saw that I spent a lot of time in the gym. They wanted to be a part of this competition, so they sponsored me. I was thrilled. In the past, I spent much time on stage in gymnastics and dance. I loved to choreograph, and I was good at it. It came naturally.

I was in my element, preparing my individual routine. I chose Janet Jackson's song, "Control." It was the 80's, and it was a very popular song. Who didn't like to dance to Janet Jackson?

The day finally came for the competition. I had a great time and won the Miss Lake Tahoe bodybuilding show. I really tore it up in my routine with my handstands, moonwalk, and dance moves. All my dance and athletic training paid off. They took my picture and put it on the front of the Lake Tahoe magazine.

Page 12A   Tahoe World   Thursday, December 4, 1986

Tahoe City bodybuilder Cindy Taylor poses during part of a routine at a regional championship in Reno in which she claimed second prize in her first competition ever.

Cindy Places Second in Her First Bodybuilding Competition: Reno, Nevada Regional Championship

My gym family and Chase were excited and happy for me. They got my bodybuilding picture blown up. They framed it and hung it in the gym, along with my trophy. The owner of Iron Works was named John. He offered me a job at the gym, which I accepted. I would be a personal trainer and help others grow stronger and use weights correctly.

I had always wanted to own a boutique. I rented a space in the gym and had my own boutique. I sold workout clothes, leg warmers, tights, headbands, and all the things we used to wear in the 80's.

With the boutique and bodybuilding, I then spent more time in the gym. I was submerged in the bodybuilding culture and community.

Bodybuilding is a practice for people who wish to transform their body structure through intensive muscular exercise and nutrition. There are definite pros and cons to this sport.

Pros

1. Bodybuilding helps you increase self-discipline.
2. Bodybuilding helps you stay active.
3. Bodybuilding helps boost your confidence.
4. Bodybuilding helps you learn proper nutrition.
5. Bodybuilding helps you develop motor control.

Cons

1. Bodybuilding can cause stress on your joints and tendons over time.
2. Bodybuilding can increase your risk of injury.
3. Bodybuilding can cause you to become obsessed over the size and shape of your muscles.
4. Bodybuilders can engage in risky behavior to meet their goal of getting bigger and leaner—such as steroid abuse.
5. Bodybuilding can be time-consuming and expensive.

Tahoe City Bodybuilding Competition

I enjoyed the attention I received as a bodybuilder. I ate, drank, and breathed bodybuilding. I was intensely focused. This brought me offers to do fashion modeling. I was asked to model in a high-end fashion show in Squaw Valley. It was my first modeling show, and I really did well at it. I know that working out and being in shape gave me a lot of confidence and opened doors for me.

Meanwhile, my personal life with Chase was not going well. He traveled a lot, but I knew a long time ago we were not meant to be together. We always fought. Plus, I didn't love him even though he was a great guy. However, I believe he was in love with me. He gave me a gold nugget ring with a diamond (not an engagement ring), which gave me the idea that he was serious.

I realized there was something not right with Chase. He shared that when he was about 12 years old, he found stacks of pornographic videos in his father's closet and began to watch them. I believe that opened him up to a perverted spirit of pornography.

I see now that spirit had been transferred to me. I was not the same since I had met Chase. I became uninhibited about my body. Modesty went out the window. I had worked hard for this body, and it was time to show it off. I can see now how that spirit causes many problems in someone's life.

Summer was coming, and Chase was going to spend it helping his parents' business run canoe sightseeing trips in New England. I did not want to go with him. I had a friend named Caroline, who I went to high school with. She was sharing a condo with a couple of her friends for the summer in Hilton Head Island, South Carolina. She had an extra bed in her room and invited me to spend the summer with her.

13

HILTON HEAD SUMMER

The summer in Hilton Head was one to remember! Caroline and I were close in high school. I could tell she noticed that I had changed, and not simply the size of my muscles. I was like a bird let out of a cage. I was not with Chase. There was no one there to hold me back. I was free to have fun and to be me.

I was still focused on bodybuilding and worked out a lot. I now had confidence and tried out for every competition on the Island. I paid most of my rent and food from winning competitions.

Growing up, I didn't spend much time at the beach. Even today, if you ask me whether I prefer the mountains or the ocean for a vacation, I will say the ocean every time. Spending the summer at the beach was beautiful. The atmosphere was electric with fun and sun. I loved the smell of suntan lotion and the feel of sand between my toes.

As a swimmer, I really enjoyed water and body surfing. I loved how refreshed I felt after spending a long day in the sun and waves. I delighted in getting a sun-kissed tan and the smell of ocean salt. I appreciated the sound of the waves and seagulls.

A lot of kids right out of high school or college move near the ocean for the summer. There are a lot of jobs at night in restaurants and bars. The money is good, and the nightlife is too. This was the goal of many people my age. Go to the beach during the day and work at night. I got a job at a local pizza place on the oceanfront. *Guido's Pizza*. I did not have a car. It was perfect because it was close enough that I could walk to it.

I recall walking home one night. I had worked the night shift at Guido's. One way to get to my condo was to walk on the beach for about a mile and then take a shortcut through the trees and other houses.

At that time, walking home alone was not a fearful thing. It was safe. I specifically remember walking near the ocean under a full moon. The reflection of the moon shone on the waves, and the weather was perfect. I was not a Christian, but I felt the presence of God in His creation.

I always knew there was a God. As a little girl, I was close to Him. Many times on my journey of life, I have visited and experienced beautiful places. Even though I was not walking close to God, I always appreciated His beauty.

There were a lot of activities and contests that summer at the beach. No one was bored. There were many nightclubs and places to have fun. I signed up for the Hot Body contest that was on the beach.

The people who sponsored the Hot Body contest put up a makeshift stage on the beach. The girls who entered the contest had to show off their bikini bodies. There were large crowds of young people drinking and having a good time. It was my turn to get on stage. I wore my white bikini and white heels and did my handstands, flip, and moonwalk.

I won the Hot Body contest. That started my summer off with a bang. I got attention from guys and even girls who complimented me. The summer was full of days at the beach with friends, throwing frisbees, and flirting with cute guys. Because I did not make enough money at Guido's, I entered other contests. I once won the Hot Legs contest at the Holiday Inn. I also won several dance contests.

I suspect the owner of Guido's Pizza was probably wealthy. I could tell he liked and trusted me. He had a brand-new, shiny gold Porsche. He was going on a business trip with his friend and needed a safe place to keep his car. I told him he could keep it at my house. He took me up on that offer.

There was a famous nightclub on the Island called *Jim's Paradise*. My friend, Caroline, introduced me to the bartenders and employees. They were popular. One was a swimsuit model named Irene, and one of the guys was a bodybuilder named Chuck. I looked up to Irene because she was on a poster as a swimsuit model.

One weekend all my friends and I were going to Jim's Paradise. I decided to drive to the club in the Porsche. Jim's was a restaurant during the day; at night, it was the hottest party spot on the Island. As you walked into the nightclub, there was a huge bar and lots of space to stand or sit. There was also a large outdoor patio and a dancefloor in the back room. The place was wall-to-wall people almost every night.

After a few hours of drinking and dancing, I saw my new friend, Irene. She was all dressed up. I wanted to hang out with her. I told her about the Porsche I had in the parking lot and asked if she wanted a ride. Of course, she did! We had a great time riding around. I remember the music blaring and the sunroof opening. The wind blew through our hair on that beautiful beach night.

I wasn't drunk, but I had been drinking. As I look back, I can see the signs that this was the time in my life when alcohol started impairing my judgment. I heard somewhere that most people who are in bondage to alcohol do not die or get hurt by the alcohol itself but by the stupid things they do while they are intoxicated.

My friend Irene was from Hilton Head. She told me of a few back roads we could drive on. I was having a blast and driving faster and faster. We picked up speed on a dark road. I was thinking, "Wow, I am on an island in a gold Porsche with a swimsuit model and having a great time." The weather was perfect. I was tan and in shape and free. Life couldn't get any better.

I had a hard time seeing the sudden curve. The beautiful Porsche went flying off the road and into a mud-filled ditch. I heard the loud racket under the car as it was scraping along the ditch. Oh no, what just happened? I was in shock. My adrenaline pumped hard. We both got out of the car to assess the damage. It was too dark to see anything. I am grateful that no one was hurt. Again, God was with me!

I remember being scared. My boss was going to come home tomorrow. The damage was done to the underside of the car. What was I to do? I was 22 years old, and nothing like this had ever happened to me. I had no insurance or way to pay. My friend told me to play dumb and tell him I did not know what happened. I was not raised that way. I was raised with integrity. So, this complicated things.

When my boss got home, I gave him the car. The next day, he approached me about what happened to the underneath of the car. I told him I did not know. I think we both knew it was me and that I was scared and lying to save myself. He did not say another word. I am sure you are not surprised that I resigned from my job at *Guido's Pizza*.

I got a job at *Jim's Paradise* as a hostess for lunch and later as a waitress. I was now in the popular crowd. I had a couple of affairs that summer and tried cocaine. As I look back at my summer in Hilton Head, I realize I had ten more years of alcohol addiction to go before I ended up in rehab in 1995.

Jim's Paradise held a tan contest every Friday night. All the winners came together for the finale at the end of the summer. The person who won that final contest won a trip for two to Acapulco, Mexico. I really wanted that trip.

Trip to Acapulco, Mexico

I won the tan contest one Friday night. That made me eligible to come back for the big contest at summer's end. The time had come, and most people did not show up for the final contest because they were tourists and were not able to make it. I was able to be there, and I won the trip to Acapulco for two. I was elated. I had never won anything like that before. Since I was still living with Chase, I took him on the trip.

14

COMPETITIONS AND POWERLIFTING!

The summer in Hilton Head was coming to an end. It was time to fly back to my life in Tahoe City. I was leaving the freedom I had in Hilton Head. I really enjoyed the beach, the fun, and the sun! Now, it was time to go back to Chase, who I knew was not compatible with me. I was, however, excited to get back to the gym and start preparing for my next bodybuilding show in Oakland, California.

The shift from the East Coast beach to the West Coast mountains was a big one. As I got back to my routine in the gym, Chase was gone a lot as a ski coach. It seemed like the arguments between us kept getting worse.

Chase and I did take time out to go on the Acapulco trip. I loved the beauty of the beaches and watching the cliff divers. I enjoyed the aqua color of the water as we swam on the beach. Acapulco was full of nightlight and wonderful food. I wanted to experience the nightlife in a bigger way. I was wide-eyed and wanted to explore. Chase was not like me at all, and in fact, he was boring. I was disappointed.

I know that Chase could see the potential in me and was very concerned about my drinking and partying habits. I found a letter he wrote years later where he shared his concern. He had said that he loved me and saw great potential in my life. When he saw me drunk one night, he said it was hard for him to see me intoxicated and throwing away my life. Well, he wasn't wrong. I did not see that back then. I was young and thought he was the problem.

I had two very good friends at the gym in Tahoe as I was training for my bodybuilding show in Oakland. One was Al. He was originally from Lebanon. The other friend was Anne, who was from the San Diego area. We saw each other every day and just hit it off. Al became one of my best friends. There was not an unhealthy attraction between Al and me. We did everything together. Al was also working out a lot and became a trainer in the Iron Works gym.

After much preparation, I was finally on my way to my second bodybuilding show in Oakland. I had my new fluorescent green bikini. My routine was intact, along with my tan. I was ready to go and felt confident. Chase and Al went with me. It was a good show with lots of competitors. I was in the all-natural group, which means we do not do steroids.

I felt as if I had done my best. I tied for first place with another girl. We were similar in body type and symmetry. I believe the judges had a hard time deciding between us. In the end, I took home second place in my group. The girl who won first place barely beat me. I was fine with it. It was a great experience, and I got to bring home a few more trophies.

I went back to training hard in the gym. I knew I needed to gain more muscle mass, so I began powerlifting. Bodybuilders work out to gain muscle mass in the off-season. They lift heavier weights and do fewer repetitions. When it is time for a competition, the bodybuilder starts lowering calories, losing weight, and doing higher aerobic activity. This is so the muscles can be seen and observed.

Powerlifting is a strength sport that consists of three lifts: squat, bench press, and deadlift. I trained and signed up for a few power-lifting competitions. In the completion, the athlete attempts a maximal weight single lift.

During the competitions, we had to wear these very strange powerlifting outfits called singlets. They fit tight and were made of synthetic textiles to allow for support. This helped the judges see that your squat was in a certain depth.

We also had to wear belts. A little-known fact is that powerlifters use ammonia. I thought it was strange and never used it. The ammonia is used in a competition as a stimulant to increase arousal and to offset fatigue.

I did not compete in powerlifting for a long time, but it did help me gain muscle mass and take me to the next level. I had very strong legs, so I was able to squat over 300 pounds and deadlift over 350 pounds. I have long arms, so my bench press was only 140, but it's still good. No wonder I need a good chiropractor now! I won a couple of powerlifting shows and added to my trophy collection.

I was focused on my bodybuilding, on training others, and on my boutique. This took a lot of time, but I had great friends like Al and Anne, who were going in the same direction. I had no car, so I saved up and bought a bright red scooter for seven hundred dollars. It was a little smaller than a motorcycle. It was perfect, and I loved going about town on that scooter.

15

SUMMER IN SAN DIEGO

The year went by quickly, and another summer was approaching. Chase was going away for the summer again. He was going again to help his parents run their summer canoe trips in New England. My friends, Al and Anne, and I really wanted to go somewhere for the summer to focus on bodybuilding. Anne had once lived in San Diego. She mentioned there was a Gold's Gym in that area that was owned by a well-known bodybuilder.

Anne suggested it would be a great place to train during the summer. She said many well-known bodybuilders worked out at that spot. Gold's Gym was a hotbed of training for many famous bodybuilders in the 80s, especially those who wanted to compete.

I had a vision of what I wanted to look like in my bodybuilding career. I was going for it. I was looking forward to spending the summer in San Diego at Gold's Gym. I knew the environment would be inspiring. We would be surrounded by a lot of like-minded people.

They say that bodybuilders partake in risky business to gain size and shape. It's also to win bodybuilding shows. This was true in my case. It happened little by little. I was not using steroids at the time, but that was coming.

Anne found a cute little house for us to rent near Gold's Gym. It was in Cardiff-by-the Sea, which is a little north of San Diego. It was perfect for us. I borrowed Chase's car for the summer and took off for San Diego. We were on a new adventure. The plan was for all of us to get part-time jobs and train the rest of the time.

We finally got settled into our new place. As we explored the new sights, I was amazed at the beauty of the Pacific coast. I was surprised at how different it was from the East Coast beaches of South Carolina, where I had spent the summer before in Hilton Head.

The beaches, cliffs, surfers, and the temperature of California were much different than the East Coast. The beaches on the east coast were more humid. I don't really know how to describe it, but the people and food were different, as well as other things in general.

We quickly started training at Gold's Gym. It was as good as we thought it would be. The atmosphere was electric. The gym was huge and had lots of top-notch equipment.

We started looking for jobs and getting used to our new surroundings. I was young and excited to be in this new place. I was fearless and curious. Yet I remember a sense of loneliness. I look back and see that I was searching, searching for purpose and peace. It would be a while before I found it.

It was time for me to get a job. I searched to no avail. I went up and down the coast to every restaurant, coffee shop, and bar, and nothing. I was frustrated. Fortunately, my friend Al had more success than I did.

He found a newspaper advertisement saying a company was hiring for a Strip-a-Gram position. The advertisement said you had to look good in a bikini and you needed to have your own vehicle. I was curious. I had a great body that I had been working on for a long time. I had won bikini and bodybuilding contests. I wanted to take the next step.

I called the company. They said to come in for an interview at a local motel. It sounded a little shady, but I had Al with me. So, I signed up for an interview. Today, anything like this would be dangerous. It's a different day.

In the early 80's, I had no problem crossing the country with my friend and camping in a tent along the way. I had no problem hitch-hiking in Vermont when my car died. It was dangerous, but nothing like it is today. Things have really changed.

The day of the interview arrived. I was grateful that Al came with me to the motel. I was required to bring a bikini with me. The man in charge explained to me what a strip-a-gram was. I did not feel in danger. He asked me to go into the bathroom and change into my bikini. I felt safe because Al was in the car waiting for me. I guess I passed the test because he hired me.

He told me the next step was to go to Hollywood to be trained. I drove to Hollywood that week. The group of Strip-a-Gram employees trained me and explained to me how it all worked.

In the 80s, we did not have cell phones. We had beepers. When the Strip-a-Gram office received a request for a girl, they beeped me. I'd call back and receive instructions. One day, I received the address of the party and the name of the person in charge. I arrived disguised as a secretary. I had a bikini underneath a longer skirt. I also wore a nice white blouse.

I had a box that looked like a big gift. Inside the box was recorded strip-tease music. At the magic moment, someone would call me up, and I'd place the gift box next to the lucky victim. I'd open the box, turn on the music, and do my strip-tease dance. The place would go wild. The lucky victim, however, often was beet red with embarrassment.

The hosts of these parties were nice and professional. It was not a sexual thing for me. I was an athlete and liked to make people laugh and have fun. It seemed to be a good fit.

As I look back now, a Scripture comes to me. Proverbs 14:12 says, "There is a way that seems right to a man, but the end thereof is the way of death." It leads to destruction. The Bible says that sin's pleasure is only for a season (Hebrews 11:25). Then it is over, leaving us bitter, and finally, it destroys us. A day of reckoning always comes.

I was young and unprepared for the world and all it had to offer. It was ready to chew me up and spit me out. I really did not feel I was doing anything wrong or that I was violating my conscience. I had a good body, and I was going to use it to make money so I could train and continue my vision.

I was probably justifying that the Strip-a-Gram was fine because my body wasn't totally uncovered. Hey, I had on a bikini! And I was bringing fun and laughter to the party.

I put over 10,000 miles on Chase's car that summer in San Diego while traveling for Strip-a-Gram. I got to see a lot of San Diego and the surrounding areas, and San Diego got to see a lot of me. We did not have GPS back then. I bought a nice thick map of San Diego and became a professional at reading it.

Some of the positive places that really stuck out to me were the sunsets in La Jolla and the Top Gun Training Center in Miramar. I was sent to do a job when some of the Top Gun pilots were retiring. I had jobs at construction sites and at beautiful homes. On Saturday nights, I would have a job or two in the downtown San Diego area. Al would come with me, and we would go to the popular dance clubs afterward. San Diego is a bustling city.

While we lived in the area, we went to the famous San Diego County Fair on the Del Mar Fairgrounds. Many know the Del Mar Fairground for horse racing.

I remember it being big and full of wild rides, concerts, and lots of food and action. I was an adrenaline junkie back then. I wanted Al to go on one of the fast rides with me. He kept saying, "No, no, I don't like those fast rides."

I finally got him on one of the rides, and I remember it like it was yesterday. I even remember the song playing. It was *Smooth Operator* by Sade! In the middle of the ride, I could see his face turning pure white. It wasn't a smooth ride for Al. He got off and went right to the trash can to throw up. He really was a good friend!

The summer was almost over, and it was time to go back to Tahoe City. San Diego was good, but it opened the door to Strip-a-Gram. This took me to other places in the future that I did not want or need to go. It was a gateway to the dark side.

16

MEETING JURGEN

Anne, Al, and I accomplished what we needed in San Diego. When summer ended, we headed back to Tahoe to continue working and training. I remember the intensity of the snow that year.

When it snows in Tahoe, sometimes there is so much snow that you cannot even find your car. The snow is much different in Tahoe than it is in Vermont. In Vermont, it is cold and Icey. In Tahoe, the snow is fluffy. You could ski in your short sleeves and shorts if you wanted to.

One day in August 1987, I was taking Chase to the San Francisco airport. He was going to one of his coaching jobs. He traveled a lot, and we fought a lot. The same week Chase was out of town, I had a life-changing experience.

Jurgen, my future husband, came into Iron Works gym to work out while I was working there at the front desk. He was also a bodybuilder and was two years older than me.

He was raised in a small town in Southern Germany. He came to the US because a friend of his from Germany lived in Arizona. He invited me to stay with him. Jurgen was there when he got a call from his good friend, Manfred. He was from Austria and had been Mr. Universe at one time. He had been Jurgen's training partner, too.

Manfred was host, tour guide, and trainer for a group of German bodybuilders for a few weeks in LA. He asked Jurgen to help him. Manfred, Jurgen, and the German bodybuilders would tour LA and work out in different gyms, such as World's Gym or Gold's Gym. Sometimes, they worked out with famous bodybuilders.

Meanwhile, as they took a break from the tour, a friend gave Jurgen a key to a cabin in Lake Tahoe. Jurgen and two friends from the bodybuilding tour drove to Tahoe. They found the cabin and got settled. Jurgen and his friends were looking for somewhere to work out.

They came to Ironwork's gym, where I was working. When I first saw Jurgen, I was shocked because I knew most people who worked out at that gym. I had never seen him before. He took my breath away. I remember it like it was yesterday. He was a blue-eyed, blonde body-builder and wore blue workout tights. His personality seemed reserved.

He asked me with a strong German accent if he and his friends could work out. My heart started beating fast. I was sweating. I charged him ten dollars. That was a lot of money to work out back then. He still talks about that after 37 years.

After their workout, they asked if there was a beach near where they could play volleyball. I directed them across the street to Kings Beach. I asked Jurgen if he would like me to be his tour guide for Tahoe and Reno. He said yes. I called someone to take my place at work and met them at the beach.

Jurgen and I spent that week together in Tahoe. It is a week I will always remember. We were so much alike. It was as if we had known each other for a long time. We rode around on my red scooter. We took long walks. We played tennis. We ate ice cream at the local ice cream stand. We rented a motorboat on the lake.

Cindy's and Jurgen's First Meeting: Lake Tahoe

I can still remember how fast that boat was moving. Our faces were in the sun, and our hair blew in the wind. Could this be love?

After our whirlwind week in Tahoe, Jurgen had to go back to LA to finish the tour with the German bodybuilders. When he left, my heart felt empty. Something deep had happened in my soul. I knew I needed to leave Chase and get my things out of his apartment.

This was a very confusing and emotional time in my life. I shared with a friend what I was experiencing. She owned a house that was not far from me. She said it was empty most of the time because she was traveling a lot for work. She said I could move my things into her home for a while until I figured out my next move.

I took her up on this offer. I packed all my things and started moving out of Chase's apartment. Chase and I had been together for over three years. I still had to pick him up from the airport in a few days and tell him that I had moved out and found someone else.

The emotional and physical stress was overwhelming. I had never heard of a panic attack until then. One day, as I was moving my things out of Chase's apartment, my body started shaking uncontrollably. I was pretty in tune with my body. This frightened me.

I called the hospital and talked to a nurse. She thought I was having a panic attack. She said my body was reacting to the overload of my emotional state. I also went to get a full blood test because it freaked me out so much. The blood test was fine. My body started to calm down.

The day came when I had to pick Chase up from the airport and tell him I had moved out. That was hard. He was not happy. He tried everything to win me back. I have always had a compassionate heart and never wanted to hurt anyone. I can see now that this split was something that needed to happen.

It was not long before Jurgen came back to see me again for the second time. He stayed with me in my new place. We had a wonderful time again. Now what? He had to go back to Tucson, where he lived, because he had a job there as a painting contractor. We were thinking of a plan to be together. When he left, we were strategizing a way for me to come to Arizona.

I was still working as a trainer at Ironworks Gym when Jurgen left for Arizona. I was trying to figure out what the next move would be for me to be with him. I had no car, and he did not have a place for me to live. Jurgen and his friend, Rick, were both renting a room in the same house in Tucson, Arizona. There was not a lot of extra room for me.

I remember talking to one of my clients, who was an older, elegant, and wise woman. She contracted polio as a young girl and had a limp. One day, while I was training her, I opened up about my situation with Jurgen. I remember her saying, "Follow your heart." I trusted her and her wisdom. I knew I had to move forward and take a leap of faith.

At the same time, there was a girl named Hope at Ironworks Gym. She was involved in the aerobics classes. Hope had black hair and ivory skin. Her appearance looked to be of Asian American descent. She heard that I wanted to move to Arizona. She approached me and told me she had a steady boyfriend named Tony in Tahoe. She had shared with Tony that she wanted to go to Arizona for a while and study yoga. She wanted to open her own studio someday. We talked, and her boyfriend offered to take Hope and me to Arizona.

The plan was that we would load our stuff in Tony's car. He would drive us to Arizona. Hope told him she would stay for six months and then return to Tahoe to be with him. She promised him that he could visit regularly.

I told Jurgen our plans. He was excited. He reassured me that he would find us a place to live. We finally set a date for the big day. I said "Goodbye" to all I had built through the years in Tahoe. I quit my job at Ironworks and shut down my boutique. I said goodbye to my friends, Al and Anne, and many others. It was bittersweet!

Once in Arizona, Jurgen and I got to know each other. Was it lust or love? Whatever it was, it was something different. Fast forward to today. Jurgen has been my husband for 37 years now. It was not all peaches and cream. There were some very difficult times that I will share with you with Jurgen's permission. I will also share the wonderful victories.

God loved Jurgen and me so much that He put us together. Even when we were not serving Him, God had His hand on us. We were young and naive. The devil did all he could to separate us and kill us because he knew we would be a threat to him.

Our testimony is how we overcame many obstacles. Hopefully, it will encourage you never to give up. I am sharing our story to spread the hope that Jesus Christ can heal and restore. He can repair what was broken. He can do the miraculous. He did it for us, and He can do it for you.

17

HEADED TO TUCSON/TRIP TO VEGAS AND GETTING MARRIED

The big day had come. Hope and I packed all our things into Tony's car. His car was loaded door to door with our stuff. It was a 14-hour drive. We were going to drive through the night. Hope was in the front seat with Tony. I barely fit in the back seat with all our stuff. I remember the feeling of excitement about my new life. I also knew this leap of faith could be risky.

After we had been driving for some time, the day turned into dusk. When I think back, I can recall the beauty of the sun going down on the mountain range as we drove closer to Arizona. I was leaving my past and stepping into a new future. I had no idea what was ahead. I am grateful God was with me, even if I did not know or acknowledge it at the time.

We finally made it to Tucson after a long trip. We met Jurgen and transferred our things into his car. Tony met Jurgen as he dropped us off. Hope and Tony said their goodbyes. We were able to stay with Jurgen and Rick for a while in their small apartment until we found our own place.

I came to find out that Jurgen had a friend who had a house for rent in Tucson. We immediately jumped on it. Hope and Rick started to date, which was not surprising. The four of us spent a lot of time together. We finally moved into the new rental property. It was nice and spacious. Jurgen and I were ready to start training together to prepare for the bodybuilding shows ahead. We were excited to do couples' competitions as well as our individual competitions.

A few shows we were focused on were the Copper Classic, Mr. and Mrs. Tucson, and the Southern Arizona Classic. It was time to put all our energy into training and getting jobs. The house had no furniture. We slept on the floor on a single mattress. The only thing we really owned was Jurgen's big, blue Buick. We nick-named it the Beast. We had many memories of that blue Beast.

Right after we moved into our rental house, Jurgen got a call from his mother and sister, Elke, who lived in Germany. Jurgen was the oldest of two sisters and one brother. His mother and sister had some time off. They wanted to come to America to visit Jurgen and me and tour parts of the country. They really wanted to go sightseeing in Arizona, California, and Las Vegas.

It was not long after we got our rental house that Jurgen's mother and sister finally arrived. I was excited to meet them and go on our ten-day trip. We didn't have much money. Jurgen's mom and sister helped us with food and hotels. We didn't need much. We slept in Motel 6's along the way. They were reasonably priced.

We took the "Beast," the Buick, and the four of us were off on our adventure. It was October 1987. The weather was beautiful. We traveled to San Francisco. We saw Fisherman's Wharf and the Golden Gate Bridge. We traveled to Los Angeles and the surrounding areas. We visited the beautiful California beaches of Monterey and Carmel.

Jurgen's mom, Emmi, did not speak much English. His sister, Elke, did speak some English because they taught it in her school in Germany. We did not have a hard time understanding each other. If we did, Jurgen was our interpreter. We played a lot of charades, talked with our hands, and laughed a lot. They taught me some German songs. We sang loudly with the car windows down. I taught them some American songs, too! It really was a great trip.

Jurgen and I rode in the front seat of the Beast. We hugged and kissed the whole trip. Was it love? I am not sure, but we were all over each other. His mom and sister were rolling their eyes but smiling. There was chemistry between us, and sparks flew. Passion was in the air!

We finally made it to Las Vegas. There was so much action going on around us. There were lights, gambling, and all-you-can-eat buffets. There were shows, shopping, nightclubs, and much more. We checked into our hotel and later went out to walk the Las Vegas Strip. We went into a casino and gambled a little, then sat at a table and had some drinks.

After we left the casino, we continued walking, soaking it all in. We went a short distance and passed a chapel called the Cupid Wedding Chapel. Jurgen looked at me and said, "Do you want to get married?" It just seemed to flow. Emmi and Elke thought that would be a great idea. I thought, "Sure, why not!" Emmi and Elke said they would pay for the service.

Did you know that 120,000 people get married in Las Vegas every year? That is 10,000 a month, over 300 people a day. I didn't know any of that back then. I just knew I was going to get married. I said, "YES!" We rented a white limousine that took us to the local courthouse to get our wedding certificate and documents. Then, the limousine brought us back to the Cupid Wedding Chapel, where we had the service.

Eloped to Las Vegas to Marry Jurgen

When I look back at old pictures of this ceremony, I just laugh. We were not prepared by any means. I had on my black mini-skirt and a white halter top, with my whole midriff showing. I also wore black high heels. Jurgen had on a black short-sleeve shirt, blue shorts, white socks, and sneakers. This was not a formal event. That would come later.

We walked down the aisle and met a lady preacher who married us. The total amount for the wedding was $180.00. The wedding certificate was $20. The two rings were $80. The music box was $25.

The chapel fee was $45. The taxes were $10. Total of $180.00. Thanks to Emmi and Elke. No, Elvis was not at the wedding. He had left the building!

Our trip lasted a little more than ten days. We headed back to Arizona. Elke and Emmi were about to go back to Germany. It had been a great time of bonding. Now, it was time to focus on our training and prepare for our bodybuilding shows. It was also time to look for jobs.

We were now married and really did not know what that meant. I chose not to tell my mother that we had eloped. I was her only daughter, and I knew she was looking forward to hosting a big wedding for me. I was going to wait and let her give us a big wedding in the future if that is what she wanted to do. I didn't want to disappoint her.

I was raised in the Christian faith, but I had no idea what a marriage covenant was. I do now. In the Christian faith, a marriage is a covenant, not a contract. It is intended to reflect the love relationship between Christ and His Church. The Bible says in Ephesians 5:31-32: "For this cause shall a man leave his father and mother and shall be joined unto his wife and they two shall be one flesh."

The way I thought about marriage was a type of Cinderella syndrome. I truly believed I was looking for a man or a prince who would make me whole. I believed I was looking for my soulmate who would take care of me and fix me. We'd ride off into the sunset and live happily ever after. I don't know why I believed that. Maybe I watched too many Disney movies. It was a lie. A fantasy that would bring me lots of problems in the future.

18

FULL THROTTLE INTO BODYBUILDING/TITLES AND TROPHIES

After returning from our trip, Jurgen and I stepped into full-throttle training mode for our upcoming bodybuilding shows. We both had competed and won individual bodybuilding shows in the past. We had never competed in the couples' competition. That was something new and exciting.

Couples' bodybuilding competition is when both individuals compete side by side as a team. The judges look for body proportion, symmetry, muscle size, and quality of muscle, including density and separation. The judges also look to see if your physiques complement each other. We were required to do a routine to music. We were also judged on the mandatory poses. The judges look to see if the routine is smooth and well-choreographed. Rhythm was not Jurgen's strong suit. I am grateful for all my years in dance and gymnastics. It helped.

While we trained at the gym, I met a lot of Jurgen's friends. There was one girl who got a lot of attention. She caught my eye. Her name was Terry. She was a professional bodybuilder, and she looked great. I approached her and asked if she would meet me for lunch. I asked if she could possibly be my mentor or give me some tips.

When we met, she told me about a mild steroid that really helped her get ripped for her competition. She said it was like a diuretic. She said it would not harm me because it was so mild. I believed her and took her advice. I was to start taking it about one month before my show.

I had experimented with drugs in the past. It did not concern me. I was on a mission, and I was not thinking of the consequences. I was focused on winning.

We were still in the house we rented with Hope and Rick. Still sleeping on a single mattress. Jurgen did not have much work. I needed to get a job. I applied for and got a job at a very well-known gym and country club called the Tucson Club. It had many racquetball courts, a full and large floor of gym equipment, an aerobics studio, a basketball court, and a full-size swimming pool.

The person who interviewed me at the Tucson Club noticed that I had worked in a gym and had done well in a few bodybuilding shows. They hired me and wanted me to open the gym at 5:30 a.m. They also put me in charge of the whole workout part of the gym.

My job was to keep the gym and weight room clean and in order. Another part of my job was to help people who did not know how to use the equipment. That was right up my alley. They put my body-building picture on the wall at the gym, with my name and job description. That was my introduction.

I was happy to finally have a job. I remember waking up early to open the gym. Because I had just moved to Arizona, I was excited about the warm weather in the winter. It was November, and I recall how beautiful the weather was. There were palm trees everywhere. It was not Vermont! No plowing the snow and ice.

Arizona summers are brutally hot. But the average temperature in Tucson in November is 75 degrees. Wow! No wonder people come to Tucson from all over the world in the winter. They are called "Snow-birds." Snowbirds are people who migrate from the colder parts of America to the warmer parts. Tucson also ranks as the fourth best place to live in the country for those with asthma and other respira-tory problems.

Meanwhile, things were not working out at our rental house. Jurgen and I decided to rent a nice apartment in a nice apartment complex down the street. This was finally our own place.

We trained hard and fast for our shows that were coming up: The Copper Classic, Mr. and Mrs. Tucson, and the Southwestern Regional Bodybuilding competition. A critical part of training is diet. Dieting before a competition is a strategy to lose fat and water. You do this so judges can see a clearer definition of muscle.

Couples Bodybuilding Competition

There's extra training that couples must do for a show. Their bodies must look alike in symmetry. They must also get their posing and choreography routines down to perfection. It was around this time that I began to take the mild steroid.

Our new neighbors were gay hairdressers. They excelled at their craft and had many awards. Jurgen's hair was extremely blonde. They gave me a hair weave and bleached my hair blonde to match Jurgen's. This was the beginning of my high-maintenance, fake, fake, fake lifestyle that lasted a long time.

To prepare for our couples' show, we had to have the same swimsuits for the posing routine. I convinced Jurgen to wear hot pink swimsuits in our couples' show. He is still mad at me to this day for that. I thought the pink suits would be bright and go with our tan and blonde hair.

Speaking of tans. On competition day, bodybuilders must have a dark tan. This is because the light shining on your muscles helps the judges see the muscle definition more clearly. So, we spent a lot of time in the tanning bed. We also painted ourselves with self-tanning paint.

Jurgen & Cindy at the Copper Classic Couples Bodybuilding Competition

Posing for judges and audiences is the main competition. Even the best bodies may be judged poorly if the pose is not done well. Therefore, we spent a lot of time practicing our posing routine. It was amazing how much the symmetry of our muscles was similar. I believe that is why we did so well.

I got stronger as our shows came closer. The steroids made a difference. People noticed that I was bigger and that my muscles were more defined. I don't know how to explain it, but I felt powerful and confident—kind of like a superwoman aura.

This was my substitute for a lack of confidence and identity in the Lord. Leaning on something other than the real thing was an open door to me trusting in a source other than God. In my case, it was my body and my looks.

It was finally time for our bodybuilding shows. We were in the best shape of our lives, and we were well prepared. The audience was full for each show. Our bodybuilding community cheered us on. There was excitement and electricity in the air. We won show after show: individual competitions and couples' competitions.

People asked to take pictures of us. After the shows, many people wanted to talk to us and congratulate us. Some even asked for autographs. It was all about us. We had both hands full of trophies. Our egos were being fed. How exciting! We could now fill our apartment with all our trophies and bodybuilding pictures. We had finally made it! Or had we?

Cindy Wins Miss Southwest Arizona Bodybuilding Competition
1987

Winning these shows was filling that inward desire to be accepted and loved by a community. It filled the void to be noticed. We felt powerful, respected, and significant. As I look back now, I see that it was all counterfeit. We were deceived! We did not know it. Let me tell you right now that you do not have to have an apartment of trophies to be unconditionally loved and accepted. You are worth more than gold! God loves you right where you are. Flaws and all.

WE ALL HAVE A GOD-SHAPED VOID INSIDE OF US THAT ONLY HE CAN fill. When people don't know who they are in Christ, they search for love, power, comfort, and community in other areas. For example, some people look for love in different sexual partners. Others seek power in money or climbing the corporate ladder. I know many people, some were my friends, who tried to fill their void and emotional pain through drugs and alcohol. The substance abuse took their lives. Too many were gone too soon. That could have been me.

The night after we finished our competitions, we received our titles and trophies. We went home and ordered two large pizzas and a large bag of M&M's. We sat in bed with our P.J.'s on and pigged out. We had been dieting for so long. That was the best-tasting pizza and chocolate I ever had!

Jurgen & Cindy Winning Couples Contest 1987

Jurgen and I took some time off from bodybuilding competitions. I stopped using steroids completely. I know many bodybuilders who died prematurely from abusing steroids. I am grateful for God's protection.

19

STRIP CLUBS, FAKE, FAKE, FAKE

I still worked at the Tucson club. We regularly worked out at Jurgen's friend's gym. Jurgen knew a lot of people in the area and at that gym. One day, as we worked out, Jurgen introduced me to his friend, Georgette. She was attractive and pleasant. We talked for a while, and she told me about her work. She said she was a dancer at the local strip club. Another common nickname for strip clubs is Gentleman's Club. The actual name of this club, however, was Bourbon Street.

Georgette shared with me that she was making a lot of money working at the club and that it was not hard work. I asked her more questions. She said they were having an amateur dance contest that Friday night. She encouraged me to try out for the contest. Georgette said she would meet me there and help me. She would introduce me to her friends.

The Bible says we have an enemy, and he is out to destroy and kill us. 1 Peter 5:8: "Stay alert! Watch out for your great enemy, the devil. He prowls around like a roaring lion, looking for someone to devour." Little did I know that I was about to take the hand of deception and dance with it.

I said "Yes" to Georgette. She signed me up for the contest. The hook was the cash. We desperately needed money, and I was tired of not having any. It all seemed right up my alley. I have been on stage since I was six years old. I have been in many bikini and dance contests. I loved dancing and the nightclubs. I had a great body, and I worked hard on it. Why not use my body to make money? My job as a Strip-a-Gram dancer prepared me for the amateur dance contest at Bourbon Street.

Jurgen and I only had one car. The night of the contest, Jurgen dropped me off. Georgette met me at the door and gave me a tour. This was an upscale club. It looked new and classy. The music was blaring, and the lights were flashing. It all seemed very familiar. Most likely because I was a big part of the disco movement and spent lots of time dancing in clubs.

Bourbon Street was a large club with new carpets and a lot of shiny brass around the stage and bar. There were three stages—one big one in the middle and two in the back. The ones in the back were surrounded by mirrors. There were many tables around with white tablecloths and a large bar that took up one long wall.

I had my blonde hair weave on and wore my fluorescent green bikini with my high heels. I had worked years on my body. I still had a tan from the bodybuilding shows. I felt confident. Yet I was a little nervous because I had never been in a strip club.

Cindy Modeling in 1990

Georgette introduced me to her friends in the dressing room. They did not bother or bully me because I was about six feet tall with my heels and had 13-inch biceps. Haaaaa!

The dance contest began. I was about the third person on stage to audition. I went out and had no problems except when it was time for me to take off my top at the end of the contest. It felt strange, but I needed money, and I was already there. I was flat-chested, but that didn't hinder me. I took off my top and ended up winning the contest and going home with a lot of money in my hands. I was hooked.

Little did I know that this business was getting ready to take me down some dark paths. It was ready to chew me up and spit me out. This industry, the sex or adult entertainment industry, has destroyed many lives. I was not going to be the exception. No, it didn't happen overnight. At the time, it looked and felt exciting and new.

What happened to me? The Bible says you can sear or sever your conscience. The conscience is the God-given moral compass within each of us (Romans 2:15). If the conscience is "seared," it is grossly insensitive. It does not work properly. It's as if "spiritual scar tissue" has covered and dulled the sense of right and wrong.

My conscience being desensitized did not happen overnight. I was not asking to be deceived, desensitized, or destroyed. The Bible says we have an enemy who comes to steal, kill, and destroy (John 10:10). No one wakes up one day and says, "I would love to be an alcoholic, drug addict, prostitute, sex addict, or maybe even end up in a drug rehabilitation program or a mental ward."

Sin can feel good and fun and exciting for a while. This can be a temporary thrill. It is an immediate hit of adrenaline that obscures the true nature of what is going on. It is pleasurable to the flesh and feels right for a short time, but there are always consequences that follow.

The Bible tells us that the wages of sin are death. I highly recommend that you take that word and walk in God's ways. It will protect you and your future. "Be sure your sin will find you out" (Numbers 32:23).

20

CASH IS THE HOOK

I started working at Bourbon Street regularly. Georgette and her friends trained and helped me. I think I was their project. I was still muscular from the bodybuilding shows. They were thinking of ways to make me look more feminine. Lace, lace, and more lace. They helped me buy lace shoes, lace socks, a lace swimsuit, and gloves. Also, bows and lace for my hair.

The clientele in the strip clubs are all kinds of men. Sometimes, women came in, too. There were businessmen doing contracts and sealing their deals. There were college guys celebrating birthdays or bachelor parties. Tucson is located near the Mexican border. I found that drug dealers with tons of money frequented the clubs regularly. So did movie stars, rock stars, single and married men—all kinds of people.

Working night after night, I began to get the hang of it. To make money, you would be in a bikini or lingerie. Guests at a table would call you over. You would then dance at that table for the whole song. Sometimes, you would be there with two or three different girls at the same time.

Cindy Modeling in Hawaii

Other times, you were just chatting during the song. The guys each would pay anywhere from five dollars to hundreds of dollars for a dance. There were tight rules in Bourbon Street. You had to stay at least three feet from the table. The men could not touch the women. You could leave a night shift with anywhere from ten dollars to one thousand or more.

Some would call this a part of the sex industry. I would say, for us girls, it was a business. A big business, and sex had nothing to do with it—at first. My friend, Renee, was a girl I had met at the club, and we hit it off. She had been working at Bourbon Street a while before I came in. She lived in an apartment near me. We became good friends. She was a great businesswoman and knew a lot of the clientele.

I would go to Renee's apartment for a few cocktails before our shift. I shadowed her for a few weeks. She met a lot of people and introduced me to many of them. She was very responsible, paid her bills, and had a nice, clean apartment with a pet.

In other words, she was normal. For instance, she would go into a shift at the club and say, "I am not leaving here without two hundred dollars." She was focused and in there for a purpose. It was fast, easy money to pay the bills.

The girls working in the clubs when I was there were not looked down on as low-lifes. It was a cool thing to work at the clubs. There were all kinds of girls from all walks of life working in that industry. I knew girls in college trying to pay their college debt off. There were models taking a year off after high school to make extra money. There were mothers and housewives, single women, and divorcees. It goes on and on.

I knew one woman who was a kindergarten teacher. She had two children, and her husband abused her. She divorced him and got just enough money for rent and food from the settlement. She worked in the strip club on the weekends to make extra money for her children's clothes and Christmas presents.

As I am writing this, I have been out of this industry for many years. I gave my life to Jesus and have been transformed and delivered. When I am writing about those days, it is like writing about someone else. When you surrender your life to Jesus, He knows how to completely heal and deliver.

When I gave my life to Jesus and moved to Atlanta a few years later, in 1997, we found a wonderful church, and we grew spiritually quickly.

I met a girl named Victoria who had a ministry to girls in the Atlanta strip clubs. Jurgen and I met with her and her husband. They asked us if we would take the lead role in reaching out to these clubs. We said, "Yes." I cannot express how powerful those years were in reaching the girls with hope right where they were.

———

I WILL SHARE MORE STORIES LATER ABOUT THE MINISTRY TO ATLANTA strip clubs. Right now, I want to give you an inside look at how and why these girls and myself ended up in this industry. I once saw on television a well-known Hollywood actor talk about his career.

He said that he wakes up every morning and is his normal self. Then, he prepares for his acting job and to become someone else while at work. He talked about living two lives. One part of his life as himself, and the other part he transforms into his character for the movie.

This is what it is like working in strip clubs. The girls have normal lives. Then, when it is time for work, they put on their outfit and step into a character. They do their job, make money, and go home. This is true until they become hooked by the industry. This takes time. It's like a slow death.

The girls get tired of men pawing at them, and they start having to drink or do drugs to go into the clubs. They are now hooked on easy money and are burned out. They look for other ways to make quick money.

The client may offer the girl to be their sugar daddy. This is where an older, wealthier man can help a younger woman for mutual benefits. Some girls turn to prostitution on the side or work at an escort service. Some do bachelor parties or travel with teams as showgirls. Other girls go to Vegas and find work there.

In the end, this fast life and fast money leads to no good end. Matthew 16 says that Jesus asked, "What good is it for a man to gain the whole world but lose his soul?"

To gain the whole world is to receive all the world has to offer: money, fame, pleasure, power, prestige. To lose one's soul is to die without a right relationship with Christ and spend an eternity in the lake of fire. There is nothing worth more than one's own eternal soul. If God and Satan are both after the souls of people, then souls must be very important. Rejecting Christ might mean temporary, earthly gains, but it comes at the worst possible price.

I have not always understood this. I was blind. I see it now clearly. That is what gives me the passion to write this book. If I can help one soul, it will be worth it.

The honeymoon phase and excitement of working at Bourbon Street strip club was slowing down. I have learned that if you want to make good money in the clubs, it helps to be unique. I was tall and very muscular. I was doing well. I remember one guy asking me if I was a Russian Olympian. I was different. It wasn't a bad thing. It set me apart and kept me away from the drama of the girls. They did not want to mess with me.

After a year or so at Bourbon Street, a new strip club named TD's opened. It was a big deal. It was the hottest, most popular club in town. It was time for new scenery. Renee and I quickly left Bourbon Street and went to get a job at TD's. The girls had trained me and made me look feminine. Now, it was time for me to get breast implants.

I searched for the best plastic surgeon in the area. This was the 80s. At that time, plastic surgery was not even close to being as popular or normal as it is now. It was just becoming popular at that time. I saved up a lot of money to get my breast implants.

I knew I would look better in my clothes. I had wanted this for years. I would also make more money at the club. I wrote earlier about being picked on in school for being flat-chested. Now I could be whole. But that was just another lie.

I got my breast implants. The doctor did a great job. I now had my blond hair weave, breast implants, and my perfectly tanned body. I was high, high maintenance. I had colored eye contacts to match my outfits or my hats and my nails. I also had fake eyelashes. The ones they glue in one by one. Then came the teeth. My friend worked with a dentist. She encouraged me to get veneers on my front teeth.

I felt empowered! I was more confident. I was noticed. It was for all the wrong reasons. It was fake and counterfeit. With all the work I was doing on myself, I became more beautiful on the outside. Beauty can be dangerous. Very dangerous.

The Bible says that the beauty of a woman is not defined by the things she adorns herself with. Her beauty lies in her character, modesty, and simplicity. Proverbs 31:30 says, "Charm is deceptive, and beauty is fleeting; but a woman who fears the Lord is to be praised." Whoops, I was going in the wrong direction. I was going to use my beauty for my own gain. I was surrounded by people that were good at that.

Renee and I always liked to do things together. She was good at getting us gigs outside the clubs that would make us money, and we could have fun doing it. She had a client named Rico, who was from Mexico and lived in Tucson. He had lots of money and was a nice guy. He might have been a drug dealer, but we never prodded.

Rico wanted to go to Las Vegas and have some fun. He said he would pay Renee and me to spend a few days in Vegas with him. He would pay for our flight, our rooms, food, etc. He did not feel like a threat, and we took him up on this offer. We flew in and met him.

We had a limousine, VIP rooms at the nightclubs, champagne, cocaine, and lots of wonderful food. We also got paid. I do remember flying back with a massive hangover. We wore big sunglasses on the airplane on the way back to Tucson. I am sure we were still drunk.

Renee and I went back to Vegas quite a few times. She knew a lot of high rollers who liked to spend a lot of money in Vegas and enjoyed having pretty girls with them. We wore expensive, colorful sequin dresses and high heels. We fit right into the Vegas lifestyle. We traveled, had fun, and made money. We did all this without having to work in the clubs.

You are probably thinking, where is Jurgen? He was struggling with his own issues, as well as with work and building his business. We were introduced to a guy named Sly. He owned a male strip club that provided Chippendale-style strippers.

This style of stripping consists of a muscular male wearing a speedo swimsuit bottom and whose upper torso is bare except for a bowtie. His male strippers were called the Male Review. Sly also employed girl strippers. They traveled all over the southwest.

Sly saw how handsome and built Jurgen was and asked him to be a part of his Male Review show. There were about seven or eight male dancers who were a team. Sly was the head of the group. He was also a dancer and a choreographer.

Jurgen was reluctant to join the group. He was an introvert and did not like dancing in front of people. I convinced him to join the Male Review because we needed money. He did.

The Male Review was well-choreographed and in good taste. Jurgen did not ever enjoy it. He had a job as a bouncer at a local bar and did painting jobs on the side. But Jurgen did love to travel. Sly and the Male Review team were about to travel in an RV and do shows on the road in the southwest and Colorado.

Jurgen was excited about seeing lots of different areas. He used that opportunity while traveling to get up in the mornings to hike and explore the different territories. The group was once asked to be on the Vicki Lawrence show back when she had a talk show.

TD's show club was bringing in Playboy models and beautiful women from Las Vegas, Phoenix, and other big cities in the area. I became friends with some of them. They stayed at my house many times while they were in town.

Rico was still my friend. He always asked me to introduce him to my beautiful friends. He appreciated me for that. He had a bunch of cars. One was a silver and blue Corvette. I asked him if I could drive it. He allowed me to use it. I had that car for over a year.

I can still recall one night after work. I pulled out of TD's nightclub parking lot with my Corvette and my hair weave blowing in the wind. The sunroof was open, and it was a nice night in Arizona.

I had my upbeat pop music blaring. I stopped at a stop light, and there were two guys in the car next to me. They were about in their 20's. They rolled down their window in such awe and admiration of me. They stared at me and said they had seen me in the clubs and wanted to say hello. They told me I was beautiful.

Wow. Wasn't that what I had been looking for all my life? To be respected, noticed, and admired. I had finally arrived. Or had I? Beauty fades. It lasts only a little while. I was at the peak of my beauty. Little did I know it was going to all come crumbling down one day.

21

BIG WEDDING IN VERMONT

My mom told me she wanted to put on a big wedding for Jurgen and me in Vermont. It was 1989, and Mom and Dad put on a traditional fancy wedding for us.

When I flew into Vermont, my mother's mouth dropped open in shock. She told me I looked like a roller derby queen. The blonde hair weave, big muscles, and the new breast implants threw her off. I think she was disturbed and concerned about me. I don't blame her.

Jurgen's parents flew to Vermont from Germany for the wedding. Mom bought me a beautiful wedding dress and a breathtaking bouquet of flowers. We had a classy rehearsal dinner. My mom and dad went all out.

The next day, I was picked up by a white limousine and driven to a beautiful chapel. After the wedding, there was a large reception with a live band, food, and the cutting of the wedding cake. My mom and dad gave us a peaceful and memorable honeymoon at a ski resort in the Mountains of Vermont. The resort was quiet because it was off-season. In my life, I have had two weddings with one husband. I tell people that I married the same man twice!

I believe this celebration was more for my mother than for anyone. As we look back, we are glad she made the effort to make such great memories. At the time, we were not doing well in our souls or lives. I have a picture of that wedding.

One picture that I had was of us getting married in the church. I could see the feet of Jesus right above our heads in stained glass. I believe that was a prophetic picture of what was to come.

Vermont Wedding - 1989

We made a covenant at the feet of Jesus that day. When we went back to Arizona from the wedding in Vermont, we went far away from Jesus. We knew about Him but did not know him personally. We had no understanding of the marriage covenant. We were in a spiritual battle and did not know it. Rock bottom was in our future. As I look back, I see God's faithfulness to us, even in our ignorance. He was waiting for us to surrender and turn to Him.

DANCING WITH DREAMERS

22

CALIFORNIA DREAMERS, SAN DIEGO, OIL WRESTLING, HAWAII

After we returned to Arizona, we resumed our jobs and training schedule. I did not know it, but one of the businessmen who worked out at the Tucson Club gym saw me working at the strip club. He told the owner of the Tucson Club that I was working there. The owner let me go. It was a conflict of interest for her. She did not want people to know that one of her employees worked at a strip club. I thought that was very strange, but now I can see their point.

Jurgen and I, by now, had worked full throttle in the entertainment industry and traveled a lot. We were growing further apart from one another. I had a friend named Tracy that I met at TD's, the new strip club. She knew a guy named Richard who owned both a girls' and guys' dance group out of San Diego. It was called the California Dreamers. We had an invite from Richard to come to San Diego to meet him and try out for the dance group.

We were thrilled because we both loved the beauty of San Diego. We drove my Corvette, which was fast, shiny, and loads of fun. This interview could give us the opportunity to dance, travel, and make money at the same time. We looked forward to it because we were burned out from working in the clubs.

The interview with Richard went well. We got the job and were now part of the California Dreamers dance group. This was something new and exciting.

We met the rest of the team and practiced the choreography. We all got very close. We had an RV and immediately started traveling and doing shows. I recall shows we did at spring break at Lake Havasu, Arizona. There were boats and drunk people everywhere. It was mayhem. We were young, beautiful, wild, and having fun. The lifestyle had not caught up with us. Yet!

In addition to our Arizona shows, we also did shows in New Mexico, Texas, Nevada, and California. Richard also had a group of girls who did oil wrestling shows at nightclubs. This was popular and brought in a lot of people and money. Richard asked me if I wanted to be a part of the oil wrestling shows. He said because I was so muscular, I would fit right in.

Oil wrestling consisted of four girls. It was like Strip-a-Gram. They each wore a bikini under a secretary or nurse outfit. They stripped out of their outfits to loud, upbeat music. At the end of the show, the audience bid on the two girls they wanted to wrestle in the baby oil that night.

The wrestling match was done in a large blow-up ring. The two highest bidders chose two of the four girls to wrestle. The high bidders spread oil in the ring and got to keep the oil bottle as a souvenir.

The girls who were chosen to wrestle that night kept the bid money for themselves. The bid money could consist of $200 to $1,000. The wrestling show was fake, of course, but it could be very dangerous because of the slick oil.

The girls wrestled for three songs that lasted a minute each. The audience was loud and had a great time. It was popular because it was different, and as a sport, everyone was involved. I tried it, and I did well. Because of my athletic background and my muscular body, I fit the part.

I practiced a lot with the girls outside of the show because it was a performance. Some matches would go well. But other times, we would come out with many bruises and sometimes black eyes. I once had my jaw come out of place. Oh, the crazy things you do in your youth.

Richard and I got along well. He got an offer for us to do the oil wrestling shows in Hawaii. There was a club on the island of Oahu that wanted us to go to the shows for at least six months. This club was near the Navy base. The clientele would be mostly navy guys coming in and out of port. It was a popular club and always crowded.

They offered our team an apartment to share and one car. This was in the city of Waikiki. Waikiki is a big city on the island of Oahu. The owner of the club said that if our show did well, he would keep us on for a year. I was excited about this opportunity and had always wanted to go to Hawaii.

Now, I was going to go back to Tucson to share this opportunity with Jurgen to see what he thought. The apartment in Tucson with Jurgen was my home base. During this time, Jurgen toured on and off with a group of dancers called the Male Review. I talked to Jurgen about the opportunity I had to go to Hawaii for six months. We agreed it was a good opportunity to see Hawaii and make some money.

The time came for our team of California Dreamers to take off to Hawaii. There were four of us girls and the owner, Richard. We got to know the area in the first few months and got into a routine. I enjoyed being in such a beautiful place, but my soul was getting darker. This was because of the addictions and party life. It was like watching a colored movie with a black and white filter.

Hawaii - 1990

I fell in love with Hawaii, the people, and the beauty of the Island. We got to know a lot of people, especially the locals. We enjoyed the nightlife. We started to become well-known by club owners. Many of the bouncers and bartenders were Samoan and were very kind.

Our team's daily routine was we'd spend the day at Waikiki Beach playing in the ocean, tanning, or going on catamaran rides. We would then walk back to our apartment and get ready for our show. We would drive to the club where we did our shows. We would be there for a few hours, shower, and get the oil out of our hair. Then we'd go home and get ready for the nightlife.

There were many tourists on the island. The nightlife was full blast every night. We found cocaine dealers. We stayed up all hours of the night drinking and dancing and doing cocaine. We did not get much sleep. The next day, we'd go to the beach hungover and do it all over again. I don't know how I survived that fast-paced lifestyle. I am grateful that I did.

The locals call the tourists *Haoles*. When the locals see that the Haoles have been there for over six months, they embrace you. That's what happened to us. We had great favor with the locals. When there were long lines to get into the nightclubs, the bouncers let us pass everyone to get in the front of the line. We felt special. We were now locals.

Our apartment was within walking distance of most places. We could walk to the gym, beach, store, and restaurants. We had to drive to our show because it was on the other end of the island.

After being on the island for over six months, the nightclub renewed our contract for another six months. We had a lot of downtime and built relationships with some of the locals. They showed us places that tourists did not know about. We got to hang out on the north shore of Oahu, where many of the professional surfers lived and competed.

We spent time with the surfing community. We got to watch the well-known surfing competitions at the North Shore. It was fascinating getting to know their culture. The competitive surfers reminded me of the hot dog professional skiers I got to know while living in Lake Tahoe.

Both the professional skiers and surfers' communities were similar. They had their own style and language. They are adrenaline junkies. Passionate about their sport. Risk-takers but very laid back. And most were honest, nice people.

WHY WAS I ALWAYS HANGING AROUND THESE EXTREME PEOPLE? THESE people on the cutting edge? I believe this because I was created to be extreme and cutting edge for God's kingdom. At this point, I was going *extremely* in the wrong direction.

Our group was asked to do a show on the big island of Hawaii. After the show, we had the opportunity to take a helicopter ride over the island. It was breathtaking. I have many good memories of Hawaii.

We got to go snorkeling at Hanauma Bay, which is one of the most beautiful water wonderlands. I have always enjoyed swimming, but this is where I found my love for snorkeling. The fish were spectacular in their colors and beauty.

While in Hawaii, I regularly hiked up Diamond Head Mountain. Diamond Head is a volcanic tuff cone that is near Honolulu beaches. I also got the chance to take a motorcycle ride around the whole Island of Oahu and saw some fantastic views.

I once had the rare opportunity to hear a fascinating story from a lady while I was having drinks at a local restaurant. As we talked, she told me the story about how she was a teacher at Pearl Harbor and was there on the day of the bombing. As she shared this experience, I knew I was hearing history. She was old when we had our conversation. She might not be alive today.

I did get to enjoy the beauty of Hawaii, but the darkness was creeping in. I was hanging around the wrong people. The company you keep is important. I was connected to people who were partiers and were not going anywhere. The Bible says in Proverbs 13:20, "Keep company with the wise and you will become wise. If you make friends with stupid people, you will be ruined."

While there, we not only did cocaine but also a drug called ecstasy. Ecstasy is both a stimulant and a hallucinogen. There was a lot of it in the Hawaii nightlife.

Ecstasy was a popular party drug. It's probably still popular. It reduces inhibitions and gives you feelings of euphoria and empathy. It makes you feel happy. *You just love everyone.* It can be harmful to your kidneys and liver. I am sure my liver was not happy with me back then. I am grateful that the human body can heal itself. I have been out of the party scene for a long time. Thank God!

Toward the end of my time in Hawaii, I got to tour some of Hawaii with the locals. They took me and my friends island hopping. It is very easy to go island hopping in Hawaii. Many people do it.

We went to Oahu, Maui, Molokai, the Big Island, and Kauai. I got to see the black sands, waterfalls, craters, and dormant volcanoes. I was able to explore the sugar cane and pineapple farms. I fell in love with the beautiful hibiscus—red and yellow. It is my favorite flower to this day.

I recall a frightening experience with drugs. One night, I was with some girls at a party in Waikiki. I remember being up high in an apartment building, and it was raining. The girls were drinking. They took a pill and told me they were going to go on an acid trip. They gave me one. I took it. Acid is also known as LSD.

LSD is an illicit hallucinogenic drug. It can powerfully distort your senses. It can change the shapes and colors of things you look at. Or it may intensify your mood or thought process. It can either be enjoyable or very frightening. I experienced a bad trip that night. I cannot express how scary that situation was.

I recall looking outside through the foggy, rainy windows. I could see people and their umbrellas. They were melting and taking different shapes and colors. The frightening thing about this situation was that the drug brought me into another dimension.

This is what drugs and alcohol do. When you are in that realm or under the influence of the substance, you are not in control. It is in control. I could not get out of it on my own. I was trapped. It was sheer terror.

There was one girl from the party who comforted me. She told me that I was going to be fine. She reassured me that this bad trip would be over soon. Not soon enough for me. Why was I experimenting with these drugs? What was I looking for? I know now I was searching. I was searching for truth for spiritual enlightenment. I did not know it then, but now I know I was looking for God.

If you want to experiment with drugs, please take my advice. There is nothing good in these drugs. And you won't find God in them. You may find one short period of pleasure or escape from the real world. This is counterfeit and does not last.

These substances and addictions will take you down a dark path. It will lead to death. Spiritual or natural death, or both. Being under the influence of drugs will make you do things you would never do. Trust me. Choose life today. Choose love. His name is Jesus. He is better than any of these counterfeits. I know from experience.

The time in Hawaii was slowly coming to an end. Some of the girls had gone home, and I was getting burned out and had island fever. Island fever is common for people who come from the United States and spend time on the island. It's a feeling of claustrophobia and disconnect from the outside world.

I needed to make a little extra money to buy my plane ticket back to Tucson. I talked to Richard, the owner of the California Dreamers. He received a call from one of the Navy Seals who wanted to hire a girl to come to Maui. They were celebrating one of the Seals' newly graduated students.

They said they would pay for my airline ticket from Oahu to Maui and back. I said, "Yes." I highly respected the military and first responders. I was raised on the military bases. I was looking forward to it.

I flew to Maui alone. One of the Navy Seals picked me up and drove me to a very isolated house on the beach of Maui. As you can imagine, I felt very safe every step of the way. I would not go alone unless I was going to be with the Navy Seals. It doesn't get much safer than being with the Navy Seals.

The men greeted me with a smile and a warm welcome. They had rented a house on the beach. I remember standing on the front lawn. The beauty took my breath away. The ocean touched the lawn. I remember the green palm trees and the warm ocean air blowing on my face. The beauty of the sunset on the lawn of that house still is burned in my memory. I pondered what it would be like to wake up to this view every morning.

The Navy Seal guys were celebrating with cake, food, and drinks, and, of course, a great view. They showed me to my room and were very respectful. I did my show and came out with a few different outfits. Then I got my normal clothes on and came out and celebrated with them like they were my brothers.

That night, they escorted me to my room. I cannot say enough good things about the Navy Seals. They woke me up the next morning and drove me back to the airport. I flew back to Oahu. That was my last show in Hawaii.

23

GOODBYE HAWAII, HELLO MEXICO CITY

It was time to go back to Tucson. I flew back, and Jurgen picked me up from the airport. We had a time of reconnecting. Jurgen was as busy as I was. There was still a great love between us, but we were living separate lives. I know he felt guilty that he could not support or cover me properly. I had not yet hit rock bottom and was still advancing in my lifestyle of addiction, traveling, and dancing.

I was back in Tucson for about two weeks when I got a call from a girl named Salina. She was from San Diego. Somehow, she heard that I was home from Hawaii and that I might be interested in traveling and doing shows. It was so much better than working in the clubs. Traveling, seeing the world, and making money were very strong pulls.

Salina was a beautiful blonde American girl. She spoke fluent Spanish and was putting together a six-month dancing tour in Mexico. She had been connected to the California Dreamers at one time. She was breaking away from them and setting up shows on her own. She liked to be the boss.

Salina worked with two guys in Mexico who put the tour together. Their names were Mario and Ricky. They rented an apartment for us near the university in Mexico City that would be our home base.

I met with Salina in Tucson to go over the details of the tour. I looked to see if this was something I wanted to do. She said that she found two other girls for the Mexican tour. Their names were Michelle and Samantha. They were both from San Diego.

Jurgen and I decided it was fine for me to go to Mexico for six months. He worked with Sly and did tours with the Male Review. I packed my bags and got my passport. Jurgen gave me a ride to the airport. I flew into San Diego to meet the other girls, and then it was off to Mexico City.

I got to meet Michelle. She was also a blonde beauty. She had three children. I believe the children were raised by their father. I also got to meet Samantha. She was much younger than me. We immediately hit it off. She became a special friend to me. Samantha was six-foot-one with her shoes off. She was also blonde and so much fun. Being older, I felt an instinct to protect and mother her.

We all got our tickets to Mexico City and flew together on the same plane from San Diego. Do you know the saying, "What happens in Vegas, stays in Vegas?" Well, this is not true. What happened in Tucson, Hawaii, Mexico, etc., did not stay there. It stayed with me.

THE BIBLE SAYS THAT WE ARE ALL SINNERS AND NEED A SAVIOR. WHEN you open yourself up to addiction and darkness, it stays with you and becomes heavy. Darkness is heavy. Sin is easy to do but hard to live with after a while. Sin makes life complicated. Godliness makes life simple. God is light and life. I thank God that I lived to find that out.

The first week in Mexico City was a shock. It was one of the largest cities in the world back then. I think it still is now. Its population is about 22 million. Wow! This is very different than Hawaii. The traffic in Mexico City was nothing I had ever experienced, then or now. There are a lot of taxis. You can only drive your car on the road a couple of days a week. The other days you don't drive, you take a taxi.

There were some negatives. There was lots of pollution and, at times, acid rain. The language barrier was also difficult. Only one of us spoke Spanish. We had to boil our water because of the bacteria. There also is a lot of corruption. It seems there are only two classes of people. The very rich and the very poor. It was like landing on another planet.

Our apartment was not bad. We all had our own rooms. There was a kitchen and living room. This was our home base. Mario and Ricky were busy planning our shows. We traveled to town after town, night after night. We partied in the morning with the owners of the clubs and continued partying after the shows. It was fast-paced.

There were also positive parts. We got to see a lot of Mexico and get to know its culture. There are many beautiful places. As for the authentic Mexican food, it was out of this world.

We would come back to our home base for a little while to rest and prepare for the next tour. We hired a maid named Tapeti. Hiring a maid was dirt cheap. We loved our maid. She was so sweet. She was trying to support her children. The money we gave her did not seem like a lot for us. It was a lot for her. Tapeti knew each one of us well. She would wash our clothes and sheets and iron for us.

I remember we hired a lady to give us a massage, which was also inexpensive. She weighed about 300 pounds. We didn't have a massage table. So, she would lay us on the living room table and practically beat us.

One day, Mario came in and said that he was setting up a photo shoot for us the next day. He knew a nurse who would like to give us free lip injections for the photo shoot. We went to get our free lip injections. They were painful. I think I overdosed on collagen.

The lady gave us huge lips. We looked like blowfish. We got into a taxi to go home. I could see us all in the rearview mirror. It was so funny. We told the taxi driver our address. He just stared at us and our big lips. I am sure you are not surprised that we postponed our photo shoot.

We had a show in Acapulco and were invited to go on a multimillion-dollar yacht. The owners owned many nightclubs in Acapulco. We had caviar, shrimp, oysters, champagne, and cocaine. We were living the high life. Of course, right beside the highlife was the lowlife. I don't ever remember feeling so lonely. This was a foreign country where I did not speak the language. This was very different than Hawaii.

There was also the sad part. So many people were in poverty. The drug cartels and the corruption of the police were real. We got to experience a lot of the good and the not-so-good. I am grateful that we were with a good team that kept us as safe as they could. If a young girl asked me my advice about going to Mexico to do shows, I would tell her to run in the other direction.

It was strange that I was one of the most stable girls on the team. I did have my addictions, but I was raised in a stable home. The other girls all struggled with bulimia and other issues. I remember after we all ate, I could not get to the bathroom if I wanted to. One by one, they would go into the bathroom and vomit all their food.

One of the girls was Michelle. She was beautiful and had nice clothes. She had expensive, top-notch outfits that she wore for the shows. She had an all-white and all-black leather outfit. The top and pants were both leather.

But we were afraid of her. You had better not touch her clothes. Her toughness came from her hard childhood. She was never hugged or loved by her mother. We would find her in the corner of her room, curled up in a fetal position and rocking herself to sleep.

24

AXL ROSE/GUNS AND ROSES

Somehow, we heard that Axl Rose and Guns and Roses were coming to Mexico City. Michelle wanted to go and had a ticket for me. I like upbeat pop and soul music. I was not so interested in rock and roll. I told her I would go if I could wear her white leather outfit. She said, "Yes." Michelle wore her black leather. We were ready for our concert.

We took a taxi. This is where my life truly passed before my eyes. As we pulled up to the front of the Mexico City Civic Center, we realized that out of about 90,000 people at the concert, we were the only white people with blond hair. The people outside the stadium began screaming, "It's Guns and Roses!" They thought we were part of the band. The crowd began to mob us and rocked the taxi back and forth.

This is where I said, "God, don't let me die like this." Our taxi was now on two wheels and then rocked to the other side on two wheels. It was terrifying. Immediately, the Mexico City SWAT team came running out with their shields and spray.

They were able to get the crowd off the taxi and escorted Michelle and me into the concert. The SWAT team stayed close to us. I have never seen so many Mexicans in one place. It was a sea of people.

Axl Rose was on stage performing. He looked out into the audience and could see the lights shining on our blonde hair. It caught his attention. He thought we might be Americans. He whispered to his bouncer to have the security guard come and get us and bring us backstage. We finally got past the ropes in the back and into the hallway, where we waited.

When the concert was finished, the security left us in Axl Rose's dressing room. Axl was extremely popular back then. He was surrounded by thousands of roses all around the room. He had champagne and pork rinds. This was his favorite thing to have after a concert.

Mexico is high above sea level, and its air is thinner. So, you get winded easily. Axl had an oxygen mask that he wore in his dressing room between songs to help him with this. He smiled at us and asked us to come in. He asked where we were from and what we were doing there.

We had a good conversation with him, and then his band started coming in. His guitarist was one of the best in the world. His name is Slash. Guns N Roses had a well-documented rock and roll lifestyle that included heavy drinking and drug use. Slash was well-known for his extreme alcohol abuse. He loved to drink whisky to the point his tongue would turn black. Slash has now been clean and sober since 2005.

We got to know the whole band. Slash was interested in Michelle. The band was staying at a prestigious hotel in Mexico City. Axl Rose invited Michelle and me to ride with the band in their personal limousine back to their hotel. We said, "Yes." We all piled into the limousine and headed toward their hotel. It was one of the nicest in Mexico City. Slash had his bottle of Jim Beam whiskey, which he was famous for.

He handed me the bottle of whiskey and asked if I wanted some. I took him up on the offer and started to get intoxicated. Here I was, riding in a limousine with Guns N Roses and drinking whiskey with Slash in one of the biggest cities in the world. It seemed cool at the time. Not so much now.

The band rented out a whole floor in the hotel. We sat around and had a few cocktails. Most of the band were tired and went off to their private rooms. I was looking around for Michelle. She and Slash had snuck off into his private room. I was a little irritated. Now I had to wait for her. It seemed like forever, but she finally came out.

Hours passed, and it was now morning. Michelle and I went downstairs through the lobby to catch a taxi to drive us to the apartment. We still had on our leather outfits. I am sure we looked like prostitutes. We received a lot of strange stares. We finally made it back to home base. Everyone wanted to hear our Guns N Roses story.

We also ran into Vanilla Ice while on tour. Vanilla Ice and his band were on tour when we were in Mexico. He was a popular rapper and dancer in those days. He is famous for his songs, Ice, Ice, Baby, Play that Funky Music, and a couple of others.

Cindy and Vanilla Ice in Mexico City in 1991

We saw his tour bus near where we had a show. We stopped by to meet him. We hung out with him and his roadies. Vanilla Ice was very nice to us. He was a little calmer than Guns N Roses!

We finally had some downtime. Samantha, I, and a couple of others went to Acapulco to one of the most beautiful hotels called Las

Brisa's. I will never forget that hotel. It's about 15 minutes from the center of Acapulco.

It is a resort hotel that sits on a hillside. They have over 200 suites that make you feel like a VIP. We were chauffeured to our suite by our very own pink and white jeep. Our suite had its own private pool with rose petals in it. The staff wrote our names on the bed in rose petals.

Samantha and I went to the beach to get some sun. It was now time to relax and enjoy the ocean. Two guys approached us with serving trays and asked if we wanted anything to drink. We didn't think anything of it. We thought they worked in the resort behind us. We ordered two Corona beers. They brought us the beer, and we began to drink it quickly.

At first, I remember the waves looked strange. They looked psychedelic. Things looked and felt different. I looked at Samantha and asked if she was feeling and seeing the same thing. She was. Between Samantha's experience with drugs and my experience with LSD in Hawaii, we had an idea of what was happening.

Someone had laced our Corona beer with LSD and wanted to watch us trip out. We stayed calm and decided that there was nothing we could do now. We made a choice to try to enjoy the LSD trip and stay together. We walked around the beach and then back to our hotel room. This LSD trip was not as bad as the one in Hawaii, but it seemed to last forever.

Even though I was on acid, I could still see the beautiful Acapulco sunset from our hotel room. This sunset was like nothing I had seen before. It looked like a gigantic, fluorescent yellow ball going down on the ocean. It was as if the sun was slowly sinking into the sea. We finally came down from our trip and flew home with massive hangovers. I am grateful that we are still alive and that God has protected us.

We got back to our apartment and heard that Mario and Ricky had been talking to the owner of a very well-known soccer team in Mexico City. Soccer is very popular in most of Latin America. All ages are passionate about the sport. The soccer team owner asked us to be cheerleaders for the team. They wanted us to model for their team and wear their outfits and logos. They also wanted us to go down on the soccer field during half-time as their cheerleaders.

The soccer stadium was huge. It held more than 80,000 people. The stadium sits at an altitude of 2,200 feet above sea level. We did some modeling and advertising for their team. We also did a few shows for the owners of the teams. We, however, were not cheerleaders. We had to fake it and just go out on the field at half-time and wave. I remember thinking that I could probably still do a front walkover, front handsprings, and side cartwheels from my gymnastic days.

Half-time came, and we had our soccer cheerleading outfits with the logos on. It was terrifying. We just went out onto the field, waved, and did a few gymnastics. The whole stadium erupted with loud roars and cheers. I don't think they were used to seeing blonde Americans as cheerleaders. I have never been in front of so many people in my life. It was very strange.

I am not sure how long I was in Mexico City. It seemed like a long time. We had some time off during the holidays, and some of the girls would go back home or take breaks. During one break, Samantha and I decided to get some plastic surgery done.

Samantha wanted breast implants, and I wanted a nose job. I was always teased for having a wide nose. I was going to take matters into my own hands. I asked the surgeons to make my nose smaller and not so wide.

Rick and Mario took us to the top plastic surgeons in Mexico City. These surgeons did plastic surgery for many soap opera stars in that area. We went in for an interview and felt good about it. Now, in my right mind, I would never recommend anyone getting plastic surgery in Mexico.

We booked our surgeries for the same time so we could recover together. Samantha and I shared a pre-operative room and a recovery room.

I was the first to come out of surgery and placed in the post-operation room. When they were finished with Samantha's surgery, they wheeled her in right next to me. We were still pretty drugged up and wrapped in bandages. I looked over and said, "Nice boobs," and she looked at me and said, "Nice nose." Then, we both went back to sleep.

Thank God they really did a good job with our surgery. During our healing time, we watched movies to pass the time. I am glad we did it together. The surgery was subtle, and no one has ever asked me if I had a nose job.

That was the early 90's. Since then, plastic surgery has gone wild. I am not against plastic surgery, but it can get unhealthy. Many people do not know who they are as individuals, and they don't like themselves. Plastic surgery does not change your inner heart. It just changes the outside. It can be addictive and destroy lives. Only Jesus can transform your heart and help you to love yourself and others.

A few months later, Jurgen visited me in Mexico. We planned to vacation in Cancun. I was looking forward to seeing him. Little did I know, the party lifestyle I was so intertwined in was taking my soul into deeper levels of darkness. It was turning me into someone I did not want to be. I was becoming empty. I could not see that at the time. I was so entrenched in it and surrounded by others who were also unhealthy.

We had a good time in Cancun. Later, after I was sober, he shared with me that he was frightened when he saw me in Mexico. He said I looked like a ghost of a person. That I was just a shell of who I used to be. He saw that the light in my eyes was going out. I was dying slowly. He did not know what to do. He felt helpless. He felt guilty and ashamed that he allowed me to get this sick.

GOODBYE, MEXICO CITY. BACK TO TUCSON!

It was not long after Jurgen's visit that Samantha and I came back to the States. We flew together to Tucson. Samantha stayed with us in our apartment for a few days and then went to San Diego. I wish I could say that now that I was back in Tucson, I was healthy, and Jurgen and I rode off into the sunset and lived happily ever after. That was not the case. Sometimes, things get worse before they get better.

While in Tucson, I reconnected with some of my partying buddies from the past. Things got worse. I stayed up for long periods of time doing cocaine, meth, uppers, and downers. I also consumed a lot of alcohol. It was as if I was self-destructing.

As I am writing this now, I have been healed and made whole by Jesus. When I look back, I can see clearly. One of the biggest open doors that brought such darkness into my life and gave power to self-destruction was the two abortions I had in Tucson.

I believe it is important to share my story to help people who might be struggling. I was in my early 20s when I first started down the wrong path. In the entertainment industry, you are surrounded by sex, drugs, rock and roll, and the consequences that go with that lifestyle. This is the time when I had the abortions. It happened a long time ago and is very blurry. I feel like I must share.

ABORTION ABYSS

The topic of abortion causes much debate and conflicting opinions. I am not writing about this topic to bring shame, judgment, condemnation, or pain. It is greatly the opposite. Through my testimony, I hope to bring healing and hope to such a traumatic and controversial topic.

While working in the clubs, I found out I was pregnant. Because of my lifestyle, I did not have the right mind to know what to do. I was raised pro-choice, but I did not understand what that meant. I did not know anything about abortion. All I knew was that I needed help.

In the strip club community, the girls supported one another. Abortion is prevalent. When a girl would find out she was pregnant, another girl or acquaintance from the club would drive her to a Planned Parenthood consultation. Then, to the subsequent abortion.

I do not remember who took me to the consultation or to the abortion. I do remember that I was scared. I was in a fog. I remember going to the abortion clinic emotionally numb. After the abortion, I stayed on a friend's couch whom I didn't know well. While I was bleeding and recovering, they gave me pain pills. It was awful.

One thing I recall clearly is that while I was recovering, I felt an empty hole in my soul. It was hollow, empty, and dark. I was crying and bleeding and feeling so alone.

I was traumatized. I believe that, subconsciously, I was wondering if I could bury or stuff all this pain and keep going. I did just that. I used more drugs and harder drugs. I used more alcohol and harder alcohol. I numbed myself so I did not have to face what I had just done. Again, this was my attempt to sever my conscience to survive. Back then, I was not aware that I was doing that. I was trying to cope.

I was born into this world with a purpose. My purpose is to release God's light, life, and joy into the world. Now I was a murderer two times over! How could this be? I took the hand of deception and danced with it.

God has His laws and instructions to lead us, guide us, and protect us. That is why He sent His Son, Jesus, to help us walk out His will. His Bible is the blueprint for how to live a healthy life. God dearly loves and cares about us. He knows what will happen if we break His laws and principles and go our own way. Isaiah 53:6 says, "All we like sheep have gone astray." This is why we need to return to Jesus.

Psalm 139:13-16 says, "For you created my innermost being. You knit me together in my mother's womb. I praise you because I am fearfully and wonderfully made."

I HAD MORE THAN ONE ABORTION. THAT WAS AN OPENING IN MY LIFE TO all kinds of havoc. Grief, pain, and psychological and spiritual stress. When women have abortions, they almost always experience some or all of these symptoms:

1. Bondage to shame and guilt
2. Nightmares relating to abortion
3. Feelings that God will never forgive them
4. Depression
5. Self-hatred leading to addiction
6. Sleep disorders

7. Flashbacks or hearing sounds of children crying
8. Difficulties bonding with her other children

IS A FETUS A PERSON?

There is an argument that a fetus is not a person but only a mass of tissue. If a fetus were only a mass of tissue without a human spirit, then I could see justifying abortion. However, I know now that the fetus is not simply a mass of tissue but rather a person with whom God is knitting together. This does not mean they are not human beings. Jeremiah 1:5 says, "Before I formed you in the belly, I knew you."

I came to realize the full weight of what I had done: *I had killed a person. My baby. Twice.* I experienced the traumatic consequences of my abortions. I had opened the door of hell, and demons and psychological problems tried to take my life.

I want to bring you good news. If you have had an abortion, you can be free from all torment. When I surrendered my life to Jesus, I developed a personal relationship with Him. I got to know His Word, love, and peace. I repented for the abortions and received deliverance from the demons that had entered. You can be free in Jesus by His blood that was shed on the cross.

It took time, of course, for me to be totally healed. It was a process. Nowadays, there is a lot of help for those struggling with post-abortion issues. Post-abortion counseling education (PACE) is helpful and offered in many churches.

One day, while in prayer, the Lord gave me a vision of the children I had aborted. They were with Jesus and being well taken care of. In the vision, they looked at me and told me I was totally forgiven by Jesus and them. They told me to move forward in my life and finish my race (my life) here on earth.

They said they would meet me in heaven when I was finished. Jesus asked me if I wanted to name my children. In the presence of God, I named my children and let them go. I released that last bit of grief and sorrow. I was healed.

I am not tormented any longer. I do not carry any shame, grief, or sorrow associated with abortions. Jesus took it all. Once I was free, I knew it was time to help others.

BREAKING THE CURSE OF BARRENNESS

After giving my life to Jesus, Jurgen and I could not have children. We tried for 12 years. My aunt took me to Ruth Heflin's camp meeting. Ruth Heflin was a mighty woman of God who walked in God's supernatural power. She used to have camp meeting revivals in Virginia.

There was a sweet couple from South Africa ministering at one of the camp meetings. They had great faith in praying for people who could not get pregnant. They prayed for us and broke a curse off my womb (which I believe came from the abortion). We went home and immediately got pregnant.

This stuff is real, folks. There is a spiritual battle going on. Jesus can bring victory in all areas of your life no matter what you have done—if you let him. My life is living proof. Choose life. Choose Jesus. He will never let you down.

I am eternally grateful that I found what I was always looking for. I cannot keep this wonderful, good news to myself. I want to let everyone know that there is a more excellent way. There is a better way! It is a relationship with God the Father through Jesus, our Lord and Savior.

27

GERALDO SHOW IN NEW YORK/MY DOWNWARD SPIRAL

There is a saying that goes, "Doing the same thing over again and wanting different results is insanity." This is where I found myself when I came back from Mexico City to Tucson. I was in a fast downward spiral. It's a well-known fact that addiction not dealt with can lead to jails, psychiatric hospitals, or death. I was on my way to rock bottom.

When I came back from my life in Mexico, I reconnected with my friend, Andrea. She was blonde and cute and had a sunny disposition. I always had a good time with her. She was an addict and alcoholic and loved to party. She had just recently divorced her husband, who was a doctor.

She had a nice house with a pool and lots of money. We were both in escape mode. We partnered together in our very unhealthy addictions. She had money, so we always had our cocaine and valium.

I was on my couch recovering from a hangover one day. I heard the phone ring. We had an answering machine, and I heard, "Hello, this is the *Geraldo* show calling from New York City. We are looking for Cindy to be a part of the show coming up." I thought I was dreaming and went back to sleep.

Later, I listened to the message and found out that the *Geraldo* show was doing a show about women in the adult entertainment industry. They were calling those who worked in the strip clubs, oil wrestlers, escorts, and more. There was going to be an audience of concerned mothers, and there was going to be a debate. Hà! Today, almost thirty years sober, I would be one of the mothers in the audience.

The staff at the *Geraldo* show heard about one of my friends who did oil wrestling. They called her to be on the show. She was pregnant at the time and couldn't do it. She thought of me and thought that I would be a good fit. She gave them my name and number. That answered a lot of questions about how they got my information.

I was up for a new adventure. I was not going to go unless my partner in crime, Andrea, came with me. I called the *Geraldo* show back, and they said it was no problem to bring Andrea. They gave me two round-trip tickets to New York City and put us up in one of the nicest penthouse suites in the area. They said they would also pick us up from the airport in their private limousine and escort us back to the airport for our departure home.

Andrea and I were excited. We were going to go kick up our heels in New York City. At the time, Andrea was dating a very rich man. He wanted to take us to the mall. At the mall, he said he would buy us any outfit we wanted for the *Geraldo* show. I don't think I have ever had anyone say, "Buy whatever outfit you want." We had a ball shopping. I believe my outfit was about $1,000. And that was in 1993 dollars!

I bought a nice black mini-skirt full of faux diamonds and a beautiful top, shoes, and jewelry. Andrea and I were ready for take-off. I think we drank from the minute our plane to New York City took off to the minute we came home. Our hotel suite was beautiful. It had a spectacular view. We were spoiled.

Bar hopping in New York City was fun but so much different than Tucson. The bar scene in New York City is out of this world. There's no end to it. You can feel the excitement and energy of the big city. Whereas in Tucson, it was lively, but nowhere near the variety and intensity of the Big Apple.

We were still drunk in the morning when the Geraldo staff picked us up for the show. I had lost one of my heels somewhere, and they had gotten me another pair before the show started. When we arrived, the staff prepped us for the show. Then we met Geraldo.

They asked me and the few others who were going to be on the show if we wanted to wear wigs so we would not be recognized. I was having fun, but I sure didn't want my mom to see me in this show. I said yes to a red wig, along with a few others who were in the group.

The show finished taping. It was all a blur. I do remember saying one thing on the show. It was not a lot. When the show was over, I was relieved. I never saw the show. It did air, and I remember a couple of people I knew saying they recognized me because of my voice. I believe it was the year 1993 or 1994.

Fast forward to my life in Christ in 2008. The 700 Club Christian talk show, hosted by Pat Robertson, asked if they could video my testimony of my transformation in Christ. They wanted it to air on their show. I said, "Yes." Three million people saw the testimony when it aired, and 689 called in for prayer after watching. Many received Jesus into their hearts and lives. What a turnabout.

28

NEAR-DEATH EXPERIENCE FROM ADDICTION

Back in Tucson, I spent more time with my friends Peg, David, and Larry. They all lived in Phoenix and worked as hairdressers. They were the ones that did my hair weaves for all my shows. They moved to Tucson and into the same apartment building Jurgen and I lived in. They were partiers. Dave and Larry were a black and white gay couple who lived two apartments down from us. We called them Salt and Pepper. Peg lived down the street.

Because they lived so close, there was always a party. We would put our money together and buy cocaine and alcohol for the weekend. Peg and I were doing more crystal meth or speed. Crystal meth is methamphetamine. You can snort, smoke, or inject it. It is extremely popular, addictive, and dangerous.

Meth is used for various reasons. It was used in WWII to keep soldiers awake. Some people use it for weight loss, such as models. Others, such as truckers and students, use it to help stay awake and alert. Unfortunately, it's abused by people from all walks of life.

The drug gives a powerful rush called a dopamine brain flood. Meth can give a person a false sense of confidence, pleasure, and energy. However, meth is pure evil. It will lie to you, telling you that you are in control and only doing this for a little while.

Then the spirit behind the meth wraps itself around your soul and leads you to dark places. Often even death. Many die from meth. It creates bad side effects, including heart issues and psychosis. Here are a few stories of how meth almost killed me.

CLOSE CALLS WITH METH

Jurgen was house-sitting in the foothills of the Tucson mountains. I knew where the keys were to that house. I knew they had alcohol in their house. Peg and I had been up for a long time on meth.

We needed some alcohol and had a great idea to get some from the house Jurgen was watching. I knew he wasn't there. I remember it was a very hot day. I had a gallon jug of water with me. I was pouring water on both Peg and me to keep us cool.

We finally made it to the empty house. They had a swimming pool in their backyard. As we looked for the key, I sat my gallon jug of water next to the gallon jug of muriatic acid used to clean pools. I did not know there were now two jugs. I was still intoxicated and out of it. Peg finally found the key. I picked up the jug of water to take a big gulp, picked up the wrong jug, and drank a lot of muriatic acid.

One of the uses of muriatic acid is to remove rust and stains from brick and concrete. Muriatic acid is a strong inorganic acid that can be used in many industrial processes, such as refining metal. Obviously, it is a very hazardous chemical. Here are four other uses of muriatic acid. I share this to let you know what a miracle it is that I am still alive and that miracles still happen.

1. Masonry cleaning
2. Masonry preparation for sealing and painting
3. Reduction of pH in pools
4. Mineral deposit removal

I started screaming and immediately told Peg what had happened. I could not talk but pointed to the jug. We were in a quiet area with not a lot of people around. I went to the outside water hose immediately. I thought I needed to put water into my body to flush out the poison. Peg went to the neighbor, who called 911.

I remember waiting for the ambulance and seeing tunnel vision. I kept slapping myself to keep awake. I didn't want to die. I wanted to live. The ambulance took me to the hospital. They took tests and kept me overnight.

Jurgen and Peg were in the hospital room when the doctor came with the results. He said I was lucky because the same acid I drank was the same type of acid in my stomach, and it equalized itself and caused no damage.

God had a plan for me. He was gracious to me. Do you think that was a wake-up call? Would I go back to doing drugs? Jurgen did not really know I was in that bad shape. He thought that I was just independent and strong.

He did not know I was doing a lot of drugs. He was living his life and was busy. He was also very naïve. I believe he was enabling me. We didn't know it at the time, but he was. He was there for me, cleaning me up when I needed it. Later, he took his hands off me and gave me to the Lord. I hit rock bottom and was able to get help.

It is hard not to enable the ones you love when they are struggling. Sometimes, it is necessary to let them go so that the person can hit rock bottom.

When I was doing drugs, I ended up hanging out with the wrong crowd. One day, Peg and I were at a party at the house of a guy named Sean. He seemed like a nice guy. I believed he was selling drugs. He had a lot of people over to his apartment using meth or cocaine. It was Christmas season, and decoration lights were up.

Peg and I were doing meth for a few days, and now we were coming down and starting to tweak. Tweaking is when meth users are coming down and out of the euphoric stage. The person can suffer psychosis, delusions, hallucinations, and an altered state of reality.

During this time, I had a screwdriver. I was going to fix something in the electrical box in the bathroom. I was coming down from the drugs and must have been in the delusional phase. I put the screwdriver in the electrical box. The bathtub was on the opposite side of the bathroom.

I put the screwdriver in the wrong place in the electrical box, and it could have been deadly. I remember a big explosion, and the power of the explosion sent me flying across the bathroom. I landed in the bathtub with my feet in the air. The explosion was so powerful that the Christmas lights inside and outside the house went on and off. Peg was screaming and ran into the bathroom and found me in the tub.

She kept screaming, "Are you alright? Are you alright?" I was not sure. I remember I could not see because the explosion was bright. I found that I had singed my eyebrows and my bangs. I was still alive!

Peg and I looked at the screwdriver. A huge hole had burned through the rubber part of the handle. It was still smoking. The rubber handle protected me from being electrocuted. It had saved my life. God had protected me once again.

2 9

JURGEN'S SPIRITUAL AWAKING

Jurgen was headed for a spiritual awakening as I got closer to rock bottom. He had always felt that he needed to prove to himself and his father that he was a man. Maybe the army was the way to do this.

In his 20s, he signed up for the German army special forces. He jumped out of airplanes, learned intense survival skills, and did all the alpha male stuff. None of that filled the hole in his soul. He was still lacking. He didn't know it then, but he would later learn that his relationship with his earthly father wouldn't be healed until he met his heavenly Father.

Now, many years removed from his army journey, he was with me on my journey. He quit dancing and worked as a painting contractor. Jurgen was searching for significance and identity in extreme sports, bodybuilding, drugs, sex, and rock and roll.

He had a friend who kept asking him to go to church with him. His name was Manny. Manny needed some work done and gave Jurgen the job. He told him he would give him an extra $1,000 if Jurgen went to church with him.

Jurgen did not want to go to church with him, but the $1,000 bribe was enough for him to agree to Manny's invitation to Fellowship

Bible Church in Tucson, Arizona. Jurgen was searching for something but did not really know what he was looking for. Neither of us were doing well.

When Jurgen went to church that Sunday, back in 1995, his life was about to change drastically. Jurgen said that when he stepped into the church, Pastor Pat and the elders greeted and embraced him. After the service, he felt something different inside. He felt like he belonged. He felt like he had found what he was looking for.

Step by step, Jurgen met with Pastor Pat for teaching and counseling. Not long after that, Jurgen gave his life to the Lord. He got baptized in the pool at the church. He also became very active in the "Experiencing God" Bible study.

The youth Pastor was named Jeff, and he played guitar. Jurgen's father had given him a guitar when he was six. Jurgen was a great guitar player. He teamed up with Jeff to learn and play worship songs.

Meanwhile, I was not doing well at all. The church asked Jurgen if he was married and where was his wife. He told them I was struggling. The whole church started praying for me! Wow, that is a lot of prayer. Prayer works. That is one of the reasons why I am here today.

30

MORE STORIES OF GOD'S PROTECTION

I'm going to share with you a few stories that will give you a better idea of what the church was up against with their prayers. They had their work cut out for them!

I recall one night, I was at a large all-night party. There was heavy drug use. Peg and I were there together. It was probably about 3:00 a.m., and we had been up for a couple of days and had drunk lots of alcohol.

I remember the music blaring and just chaos all around us. I looked up at the wall, and there was a beer stain where someone had spilled their beer. At that moment, I could see the beer stain turn into the face of Jesus. There was a drip coming down the wall. The drip turned into a tear coming out of His eye.

I thought I was hallucinating. It really shook me up. Things like this began happening more. Could it have been from the prayers of this sweet church? I believe so. Jesus was chasing me down. He was with me, and it grieved Him to see me in that shape. He was trying to get my attention, to draw my heart toward his.

Several days later (at the same party!), when I saw Jesus's face on the wall, we were all coming down off our drugs. It was about six in the morning. A guy at the party who was a crack addict asked me if I had a car. He said he knew where he could get more drugs. We were desperate to get more drugs. I told him I would drive him. We drove to a little bar with a house in the back on the bad side of town.

Little did I know, this guy was being tracked. The next thing I knew, an unmarked SUV put a light on top of the hood and turned it on. They pulled us over. Ugh! I cannot tell you how freaked out I was. This was the FBI! They had a warrant for this guy's arrest. They pulled him out of the car and handcuffed him.

They asked for my driver's license and started searching my car for drugs or paraphernalia. In the back of my car was a small briefcase with flowers on it that I had brought home from Mexico City. It had the written draft of the plastic surgery drawing that was used for my nose job.

I think the FBI thought they had found drugs or something important. They kept staring at the draft and could not figure out what it was. But they knew it had to have something to do with drugs. They came over to me and asked what it was and what I was doing with this man. I said the drawing was a draft of my new nose job that I'd gotten in Mexico City.

The whole time they searched my car, there was a crack pipe in plain sight. The guy I was with had put it on the front seat. The FBI never saw it. My heart was racing. They looked at me and said, "You look like a good girl. We don't know why you are with this man. You need to go home and stay away from drugs and these types of people."

SURE, MR. FBI MAN

They let me go, and I thanked them and went on my way at about twenty miles an hour, just shaking. I threw the crack pipe away and slept for two days straight.

I told you I was no easy prayer case.

Another time, I remember a little blue diary I was given as a little girl. I think I was about nine or ten years old. As I now read through the diary, I recall some of the writings. I remember one diary entry was about me praying for my parents and thanking God for them. I told God how much I loved Him in this little diary. This showed me that I had a relationship with him at a young age. I am thankful that God never left me.

31

BACK TO JURGEN AND THE CHURCH

Jurgen was now walking with the Lord and learning to hear His voice. During this time, he had an opportunity to go back to Germany to see his family. There was also a big job there for him to paint a whole restaurant.

I don't think he knew the depth of addiction I was involved in. He told me I had to get a job while he was away, and he would pay the rent. I agreed. Little did I know that I was getting ready to hit a very dark place.

One of the keys for me to hit rock bottom was Jurgen backing off and giving me to God. He told me later that before he went to Germany, he got on his knees and lifted his hands in the air in surrender. He cried out to God and told Him that he did not know what to do with me. He released me to the Lord. That was huge. Jurgen had stepped out of the way, giving God full permission to come into the picture. God heard his prayer.

Now that Jurgen was gone to Germany and not enabling me, there was no protection from the crazy people and lifestyle I was in. I had asked a few people over to the house. The next thing I knew, countless drug-addicted people were invading my home. I was up for days, many days. Peg was with me, and she knew I was in trouble.

I had full-on psychosis and was very sleep-deprived. When I couldn't take the craziness any longer, I kicked everyone out and barricaded myself in the apartment. I was delusional. I thought helicopters were surrounding my apartment.

At one point, I saw two men come to my door wearing suits and carrying briefcases. I turned off the lights and hid from them. Peg was so worried that she called social workers to come help me.

I was not in my right mind. Demons were in possession of my mind and soul. I was tormented. Something in me told me I needed to contact Jurgen. I don't remember this, but Jurgen said I called Germany and talked to his sister, Elke. I told her the Nazis and helicopters were after me. I can laugh about it now, but it was very dark and scary.

Jurgen's sister immediately called him and told him about the troublesome phone call. I believe God used this as a big SOS for Jurgen to come home. Jurgen did not know what to do. So, he called Jeff, the youth pastor from the church. Jeff called me, and for some reason, I answered. I told Jeff that I thought I was dying and that he needed to come to my apartment and take me to the hospital for X-rays or an exam.

32

PASTOR JEFF TAKES ME TO HOSPITAL/ROCK BOTTOM

I will never forget Jeff for the courage it took to come to my apartment. I was in a destructive state, and I am sure it was scary. I trusted him. He put me into his truck, and off we went. I ducked down the whole time in the seat because I did not want the helicopters to know I was in his truck.

When we got to the hospital, they planned to take X-rays. They wanted me to drink barium. It is normal for people to drink barium before X-rays. It's a type of dye. This makes it easier for doctors to see what's going on inside the body.

I was still paranoid and thought it was poison. I thought they were going to take out one of my organs or something crazy like that. The doctors recognized I was not in my right mind. They told Jeff about a psychiatric facility connected to the hospital and recommended it for me. They said that it would be a good place for me to rest and be evaluated.

I agreed. I was tired. I was ready to get off the roller coaster of addiction. I had been on it for a long time. I needed rest and help. I was finally ready. It took me a long time to get into this mess. It was going to take a long time to get out.

Meanwhile, Jurgen booked the next flight out of Germany. He

knew I needed him. But his mom was happy to have him home and was upset that he was leaving so quickly. Jurgen told her that even though we had not lived a normal life, he still loved me and needed to be there for me. His mom agreed.

Jeff and the nurses were in the process of getting a room for me in the psychiatric facility. Jurgen was on his way home from Germany. I had many emotions going through my mind. Part of me was happy and relieved to be able to get off this addiction roller coaster. The other part of me was terrified.

The nurse took my clothes and shoes and put them into a locker. She gave me a robe that looked like pajamas. I had a lot of questions. It was a sobering wake-up call.

Many thoughts were going through my head. I was raised in a good home. I was not sexually or physically abused by my family. I was a high school and college graduate. I had many awards, trophies, and titles. How did I end up here? I did not belong here.

Satan comes to kill, steal, and destroy, and he will do it a little at a time. I took the hand of deception and danced with it. That is how I got here. The problem with deception is that you don't know you are in it.

I looked down the hall in the psychiatric facility. I saw the cafeteria and patients in their robes. They waited for their medicine. Some of them were drooling. Some were shuffling their feet down the hall. What I was observing seemed like a picture out of the movie, "One Flew Over the Cuckoo's Nest."

When I was escorted into my room, Pastor Jeff came back to pray for me and to say goodbye. I remember this moment clearly. Jeff and I sat on the edge of my bed. He asked if I wanted to change my life. I said, "I don't know how I got here." I was just having fun and enjoying life. Jeff said, "If you want to change your life, I can tell you how."

He said, "Cry out to Jesus. Jesus can help you, and He can heal you. When you cry out to Him, He will hear your cry. He is the only way." I was in a broken and desperate place. Sitting on the bed at the psychiatric hospital, I cried out to Jesus. I said, "Jesus, come into my life. Help me. I don't know how I got here. I need you."

At that moment, when I cried out to Him, I felt darkness lift. I felt light, life, and hope come into me. As I look back, I can see how Jesus came into my life and started to lead and guide me in my healing journey. He was waiting for me to cry out to him, to choose him. When Jeff left the facility, I went to sleep. I was so tired. I think I slept for two or three days straight.

I recall the second day I was at the facility. The nurse brought a roommate into my room. She was on suicide watch. She had cut herself on the arm as a cry for help. The girl seemed sweet. I wondered why people would try to kill themselves.

But wasn't that what I was doing? With all the drugs and alcohol? I was self-destructive from the inside out. My method just looked a little different than hers. I did not want to be self-destructive any longer. I wanted to live.

Jurgen's airplane landed in Tucson. He was coming to pick me up the next day after my psychiatric evaluation. If I passed the evaluation, I could go home with Jurgen, go to church, and start healing.

Because I asked Jesus into my life, was I going to be perfect? Was I going to be completely healed immediately? No. This was going to be a journey, a process. I had taken the first step and cried out to Jesus. I went back to the faith of my childhood. Jesus was leading the way. It was a good start.

I passed the evaluation, and Jurgen came to pick me up. We were happy to see each other. He brought me home and took care of me. He did the best he could do. He cooked and cleaned for me. I stayed in my pajamas a lot and mostly ate and slept. I spent a lot of time by myself in my room. I was still very unhealthy. I felt a heaviness over my soul. I could not break through on my own. I needed professional help.

I spent years in addiction and opened many doors to the dark side. It was going to take more than just Jurgen helping me. At that time, I did not veer off into addiction, but I was not free. I went back and talked to my friend, Shawn, who was a drug dealer. He was also trapped in the bondage of addiction. I believe he wanted to turn his life around, too.

OFF TO MISSOURI TO HEAL/DETOX AND CHRIST-BASED REHAB

Shawn told me that his father and stepmother lived in Missouri. His father knew he was in trouble and wanted to help. Shawn's father offered to come to Tucson with a U-Haul, pick him up, and take him back to Missouri, where they had a farmhouse. He would detox in the farmhouse and get put on the waiting list for a room in a Christ-based rehab near Springfield, Missouri.

Shawn accepted his father's help. He asked me if I wanted to go with him. I thought it might be a good idea to get away from the people, places, and things that were in my unhealthy environment. I talked to Jurgen about it. He was not properly equipped to help me. He thought that it might be a good idea if I went.

A couple of days before I was on my way to Missouri, Jurgen and I were at our apartment. At that time, he was making payments for a minivan he had purchased. I had a nice leather jacket and a few other belongings in the van.

We heard a noise outside. It was the car company repossessing the van. They were driving off with it. I ran outside and chased down the van. I got the side sliding door open and grabbed my belongings. I threw them out of the van as it was moving.

This was a part of losing everything. That next week, the apartment manager kicked us out of the apartment because we could not make the payments. We were about to lose everything. Let me tell you, if God is calling you, do not say no to Him. This is what I did. It did not turn out well.

I lost everything. My mind, body, soul, and spirit were severely damaged. I can tell you through my story that losing everything is not God's best for your life. But if you do lose it all, cry out to him and give him your life; he can restore and heal what was lost and broken. He did it for me, and He can do it for you.

Shawn's father arrived with the U-Haul. They picked me up with my one suitcase. I said goodbye to Jurgen. It was strange, but I knew it was the right thing to do. I was ready to detox on the farm in Missouri and to wait for a room in a Christ-based rehab. It was an uncomfortable, 24-hour trip in the U-Haul. Shawn and I slept a lot while his father drove.

We finally arrived in rural Missouri. We put our names on the waiting list for a room to open at the rehab. Shawn applied to an all-male rehab. I applied at a place called the Sigma House rehab. Sigma was Christ-based, with both girls and guys. We had no idea when there would be an opening. We began the healing process on the farm.

We ate and slept a lot. This was during the time of the OJ Simson murder trials. We spent a lot of time watching the trials during the day. Shawn's stepmother, Marilyn, was kind to me. She didn't have to be. She didn't know me. But she was a Christian and knew that Shawn and I needed help. We ate so much food that she finally helped us get on food stamps.

It was strange to be in such a different place with food stamps and no freedom. I had everything taken from me. I was humbled. Every week, Marilyn took us to the grocery store. I was surrounded by big fields, railroad tracks, and cows. This was a good place for me.

Shawn and I had a strange relationship. We were coming out of the drug and party lifestyle. Our heads were still in a fog. We were not thinking straight. We thought that maybe after rehab, we would get an apartment in Missouri. That was not God's plan. That is why I tell people in rehab or recovery not to make any important decisions until they can think clearly. It takes time.

One day at the farmhouse, a package arrived for me. It was a care package from my friend, Andrea, from Tucson. We used drugs together. She was the one I took to the Geraldo show. I was happy to get a package. There were lots of yummy cookies and treats. When I dug deeper into the package, I found a little box hidden in the bottom. I opened the box and found an illegal prescription valium.

Talk about temptation. I had a choice to make. God gives us a choice to love Him and walk with Him. He does not demand that we choose Him. Then, it would not be a choice. God gave us a free will. I thought at that time that I could really use the drug to calm me down. But how could I do that and forfeit all I had accomplished? In the hospital with Jeff, I cried out to God. I would not go back.

I remember walking back to the bathroom. I had come too far. I was an all-or-nothing type of person. I could not heal my life, let God lead, and do drugs, too. I took the pills and threw them into the toilet. I chose to flush them down the toilet with my will. I remember saying out loud, "No more," as I pushed down the toilet handle.

3 4

ALL OR NOTHING/ALL IN

I had to make things right with my family. One of the hardest calls to make was to my mother. I really wanted her to be proud of me. She was not perfect, but she had invested in me all my life. I called her and had an honest talk. I was living a double life, and being honest and upfront with her felt good.

I told her I was getting help in a rehabilitation center for drug and alcohol abuse. She was kind and compassionate. I know it must have hurt her. She probably wondered what she had done wrong as a parent. I can still clearly hear her words. She said, "I love you, and you are my daughter. I am sorry that you are going through this. I cannot be there with you. You must go through this on your own. But I want you to know I am always here for you."

Talking to my mom and knowing I had her support gave me strength. I gave Mom the address of the farmhouse in Missouri. She sent Marilyn a beautiful bouquet of flowers and some money to pay for the long-distance phone calls.

Shawn was finally notified by the rehab that there was room for him. He went into rehab before I did. His whole family and I took him there. Shawn and I told each other that we would meet when we got out of rehab. That was the plan. That never happened. That was the last time I ever saw Shawn.

I completed the rehab and returned home. Marilynn and I still exchange Christmas cards every year. She let me know that Shawn was not doing well and that he was in and out of jail. You never know what or who God will use to bring healing to your life. He knew I needed railroad tracks and cows.

A room finally opened for me in the Christ-based rehab, Sigma House. I was nervous yet excited at the same time. I was ready for the next level of my healing. I had detoxed at the farmhouse and caught up on my rest. I was ready.

At the Sigma house, I had a roommate. I was also assigned a counselor. Part of the program was to put structure and order back into our lives. We had to get up at a certain time every morning and go to bed at the same time every night. They wanted us to be productive. We had to make our beds every morning, clean our rooms, etc.

Everyone in the program had to sign up for breakfast, lunch, or dinner duty. We would help clean, cook, or do whatever was needed. We also had a lot of group meetings. They were similar to Alcoholics Anonymous. A leader would lead the group discussion. Everyone would get to know each other and share what they were going through. I was stressed and full of fear. I was stuttering badly. I was not able to talk much at the meetings, especially at the beginning.

We also had downtime. We had time for recreation and playing kickball and other outside games. We had time to read or watch TV. I also remember the leaders would invite one speaker from the community each week to speak to our group.

While I was there, they had a speaker who impacted me greatly. He was about thirty years old. He was a Christian and had gone through recovery and was on the other side. *He was free.* I don't remember his name or anything about him except his message.

I look back and can recognize that the Holy Spirit was on this man. I was so drawn to him and soaked up every word of his testimony. He talked about God. He talked about his journey. He shared how God will get you through if you seek Him and trust in Him. This message gave me life. It was so encouraging. That is what I needed at that point.

I know now that that man impacted me so much because he was doing the very thing that God was calling me to do. To come out of darkness and into God's glorious light and be made healed and whole. Then, go out and share it with others. God has been so good to me. I cannot keep this to myself. I know that is why I am writing this book —to reach people. I love speaking and sharing my story. This is a passion God has put into me.

I see now that God chose my counselor specifically for me. She was critically pivotal in my life. After one week of being in Sigma House, my counselor called me into her office for a meeting. She said I needed to leave the program, get on a plane, and go back to Arizona. She also strongly encouraged me to get back with my husband and church and begin the next stage of the healing process.

Wow! I know now that the Lord spoke to her. God was using her to get me back on track with my husband and my church. I talked to Jurgen and Andrea about coming home. Andrea had a lot of money and sent me an airplane ticket.

I said goodbye to the leaders and the fellow patients I had done life with for that week, and off I went. Deep inside, I knew it was the right thing to do. I was moving forward and not looking back.

35

SOBRIETY AND MASSAGE SCHOOL, A TIME TO HEAL

When I was in rehab, Jurgen was looking for a place for us to live. His friend's girlfriend had an extra room in her house. She let him rent the room to us. The woman was named Vicki, and she was a single mother with two beautiful teenage girls. Vicki was Filipino and made the best Filipino food that you have ever eaten in your life. Her house was nestled in a beautiful area near the foothills of Tucson.

Jurgen picked me up from the airport and took me to our new room in Vicki's house. It was very nice. I have good memories there with lots of healing. Jurgen and I became active in Fellowship Bible Church in Tucson. They loved and embraced us.

Sigma House had also told me to stay connected to Alcoholics Anonymous (AA). This is an inclusive support group for people who are trying to stay sober. It is a resource that provides support and structure for recovering alcoholics.

I was loyal about going to AA. They told me I needed a sponsor. A sponsor is someone who can help guide you through the twelve-step program that AA offers. They are people who have a good amount of time in sobriety. The program insists that a sponsor is a vital tool in the pathway of recovery.

I met a kind lady at AA. She became my friend and sponsor. I liked her a lot. She often checked in to see how I was doing. We would meet at the AA meeting and go to lunch afterward. We were building a sweet relationship. Accountability was important in recovery.

While renting a room at Vicki's house, Jurgen got a job with a bathtub repair company. We had no car at the time. We were over-joyed when Jurgen got a company van. That van got us where we needed to go.

I wanted to go back to school and get a skill. As you know, in the past, I was an athlete. During those days, I received a lot of sports massages. I saw and felt the benefit of a professional massage. I used to rub my mom's feet when I was younger. Her feet would hurt after standing on them for a long period of time. Many times, she would pay me. She said that I had great hands and a good touch. That was a seed of encouragement.

I heard there was an exceptional massage therapy school close to where we lived in Tucson. I applied and got accepted. It would take me a year and a half to graduate. I was finally moving forward in life. I recognized that I was still not as free as I wanted to be. Jurgen and I had lived a dysfunctional life together for years now. We had lived separate lives on and off.

I now had a conscience and recognized that I was having trouble breaking the strongholds and habits of my past. A guy from AA asked me out for coffee. I agreed. I didn't know why. I needed help to break free from the old cycles. I was not drinking or doing drugs, but I needed God's power. I needed deliverance.

Deliverance was coming.

I thank God that He did not leave me in my mess. I started massage school. It was a great school. It was very difficult. I didn't expect it to be easy. God helped and guided me. I knew I was supposed to be there. I got a government grant to pay for the school. Plus, I was helped by friends and family. There was a great group of people in my massage school. I have fond memories of them.

Halfway through school, I got a call from my mother. She said that my Aunt Betty (my mom's sister) was helping to put on a family reunion in Kansas. This reunion was from my maternal grandmother's side of the family. My grandmother was one of sixteen children.

This is the side of my family with the deep Christian roots. I really felt the Lord was calling us to go. We knew the company van would not make it from Tucson to Kansas. Vicki offered us her car.

36

LIFE-CHANGING
REUNION/POWER
ENCOUNTER/TRUE REPENTANCE

Everything fell into place. When we left for the reunion, I could feel the Lord's presence on our trip carrying us. I did not know what it was at the time. I understand now that God was making sure we made it to the reunion. Little did I know that what would happen to me at this reunion would radically and completely change my life forever.

On the trip to the family reunion, my stomach was fluttering with anticipation to see my family. I was excited to see my cousin Heidi and her family. I had not seen her since I was twelve years old. Heidi and her family were in full-time ministry.

I was also going to see my brother and his son. My mother's sister, Aunt Janis, would also be there. She was the prayer warrior. Her daughter was Susie, another one of my cousins. She was going to be there as well. Her husband was a pastor of a church in south Atlanta.

Cousin Heidi, Aunt Janis, and Cousin Susie all went to the same church. The church was named Atlanta City Church. They were all walking with the Lord and had been for some time. I was so drawn to them. They were my family, and they radiated with the love of Jesus that I had been looking for.

We finally arrived. We had a wonderful time catching up with everyone. About two days into the reunion, I believe the Lord spoke to Janis and Heidi about me. We were at a hotel in Kansas. They called me outside. I loved and respected them both and trusted them.

My aunt asked if she could lay hands on me and pray for me. She was guiding me as she prayed. She told me to repent from the past and surrender my life to the Lord. I remember thinking, "How do I do that?" Jesus helped me, and I just released everything to Him.

God had brought me to this reunion. He was setting me up. In a good way. I had said "No" to His calling in the past. He knew I had tasted what the world had to offer, and it was not good. I did not want that anymore. I was ready to surrender my life, and I needed a little help.

The calling of God that was so apparent on my mom's side of the family was about to be passed down to me. It was about to be released and activated. It was a mantle. A mantle in the Bible serves as a symbol that represents a person's gift, call, and the purpose for which God has called him.

I surrendered my whole life to Jesus in the backyard of the hotel in Kansas. Aunt Janis and Heidi laid their hands on me and prayed. Suddenly, I felt something bubble up inside of me. It was a true repentance and a regret for all the things I had done in my life. I was truly sorry and began to weep deeply. The tears were healing. Then, I felt this supernatural love come into my heart. It was like liquid love.

I was overwhelmed in a good way. I continued to feel God's passion and power flowing through me. I began praying in tongues. A supernatural language just poured out of me. It was beautiful. Heidi and Janis were praying in tongues, too. I had never heard of speaking in tongues.

Then, I felt fire on my feet. Believe it or not, so did they! I was thrown back into the wall by the power of the Holy Spirit and was not afraid at all. I felt the fear and awe of God, but not natural fear. There was so much going on, but it was exciting. I knew it was good. I had experienced the power of darkness in my past. I believe God wanted to show me His power. I was finally positioned to receive it. I was finished with doing life my way. I was now all in.

The Bible says in Luke 5:31-32 that Jesus answered them, "It is not the healthy who need a doctor, but the sick." Jesus said, "I have not come to call the righteous, but sinners to repent." I was spiritually sick; I needed a spiritual doctor. Doctor Jesus. Acts 3:19 says, "Repent, then, and turn to God so that your sins may be wiped out. That times of refreshment may come from the Lord."

True repentance is not found in my goodness for anything I have done. It is found only in the goodness of God and His divine love and the price that Jesus paid for sinners to be saved from the inevitable consequences of sin.

What is true repentance? It's the following:

1. True repentance causes a person to make a 180-degree change in their direction.
2. True repentance requires deep brokenness.
3. True repentance creates a desire to stop sinning.
4. True repentance compels honesty.
5. True repentance commits to change.
6. True repentance leads to a practice of godliness.

MY LIFE WAS ABOUT TO CHANGE FOREVER. I FINALLY EXPERIENCED THE heavenly Father's love. That is what I was always looking for. That night, it was hard to sleep. I kept waking up and praying in my prayer language just to make sure I still had it. I wanted to make sure this experience was not just a dream. I had so much love in my heart. It wasn't normal or natural. It was supernatural love.

I was born again.

A Scripture came to mind. John 3:5-7 says, "Jesus answered, very truly I tell you, no one can enter the kingdom of God unless they are born of water and the Spirit. Flesh gives birth to flesh (natural birth), but the Spirit gives birth to spirit."

When Jesus takes possession of our lives, He doesn't merely

forgive and forget our sins. If that were true, we might keep making the same mess of life all over again. I did not want that.

When I had my encounter with Jesus, a new power entered my life. It enabled me to be and do what I could never be and do alone. Water and the Spirit stand for the cleansing and strengthening power of Christ, which wipes out the past and gives victory in the future.

A great time was had by all at this reunion. This is a reunion I will never forget. We all hugged each other goodbye. I had so much love for my aunt and cousins. I knew it was time to go back to Tucson and to our church.

I came back to the church on fire for Jesus and healed in so many ways. The fire that went through me burned a lot of junk out of my soul. I did not know that not all churches believe in or understand the gifts of the spirit.

37

BORN AGAIN/EXPERIENCING GOD/FELLOWSHIP BIBLE CHURCH IN TUCSON

Our church leadership was happy for me and Jurgen. They could see there was something different about me. They did not understand the spiritual gift of tongues (my prayer language) or the gift of intercession that came upon my life. They did not know what to do with me. That has been a theme throughout my life. However, they did not turn their backs on me. They sent me to a lady named Trudi. She taught and coached me in the things of the Holy Spirit.

Trudi had a house in the foothills of Tucson. She was a mother of four boys and loved Jesus. She had Bible studies at her home for women who were coming out of traditional churches or for anyone who wanted to learn more about the Holy Spirit and His gifts. I thank God for Trudi. She was loving and helped me to understand what was happening to me.

She told me what to do when I felt the weighty presence of God touch me. She taught me to get on my knees and allow the Holy Spirit to pray through me. I was doing this just naturally on my own, groaning and weeping. Then peace would come and overwhelm me.

Trudi gave me an understanding of what I was already doing. Romans 8:26 says, "In the same way, the Spirit helps us in our weakness. We do not know what we ought to pray for, but the Spirit Himself intercedes for us through wordless groans." Wow, what an honor and a privilege that the Creator of the world would want to use me as a vessel to pray through.

Meanwhile, we were planted at our church in Tucson, and many people began to join the services. Vicki and her children came regularly. Vicki's friend, Marlene, and her family also came. There were many more. The number of people who we invited to church was a new thing. It started when we got back from the reunion. It was the power of the Holy Spirit that drew the people through us. Many came to the church and were baptized.

The Scripture that comes to mind for what was happening is Acts 1:8, "But you will receive power when the Holy Spirit comes upon you. And you will be my witnesses, telling people about me everywhere in Jerusalem, throughout Judea, in Samaria, and to the ends of the earth."

In other words, when the power of the Holy Spirit came upon me at the reunion, things changed. I had now received the power of God to be a witness in Tucson, Walmart, or wherever I went. This is for today. It was exciting to see the Scriptures come alive in my life.

When we came back from the reunion, the Lord told me to cut off anything of the past that was unhealthy, except for one friend. That was my special friend, Peggy. She was the one I used drugs with.

She stopped by our house one day. She was in shock at the changes she saw on my countenance. She said I looked extremely different but in a good way. Peggy told me that I looked like an angel and saw the presence of God in me. She wanted to know what happened. She was convicted and wanted what I had.

At the time, Peggy still used drugs. I told her I was there for her when she was ready for a change. Not long after that conversation, I got a call from her. She had hit rock bottom in a hotel room and cried out to God. She called me, gave her life over to the Lord, and started coming to our church. It was a beautiful thing the Lord was doing. Peggy could sing, and she joined the choir. My heart burst with joy seeing her up on stage worshiping our Lord. Later, we went on many adventures together with the Lord.

Jurgen and I were now in the kingdom of God and had to learn how to grow in the Lord. We needed community, Bible study, and accountability. We needed to learn the truth of God's word and how to apply it to everyday life. This would take time and patience. We could not cut corners in our walk with Jesus. We were building a relationship with Him. We were learning to walk in intimacy with our Creator. Wow! Isn't that incredible?

We were a part of a Bible study at our church called "Experiencing God." I had a few wonderful mature women around me who embraced me and were patient and loving. They could see God's hand in my life and knew I needed to be nurtured and loved.

I was wounded. I was humbled and grateful to be alive. I would cry a lot at these Bible studies. I want to acknowledge and thank Pastor Cindy, Judy, Karen, Debbie, Trudi, and Lori. I wanted to be mature and love selflessly like they did. They were great examples for me.

Jurgen and I were on a fast-paced journey with the Lord. He was also changing quickly. Jurgen was frightened of the supernatural experience that I had in Kansas. I asked him if he wanted his prayer language, too. He was watching my life and how much I had changed. He sat down one night and told me he wanted what I had. He got out his guitar, and we began to worship. He surrendered to the Lord and asked for his prayer language, and he received it. Jurgen also brought some of his friends to the church. God was moving in me, but also in Jurgen.

The people in my massage school could also tell I was different. My eyes were literally open in a different way. I could see in the spirit realm. Psalms 119:18 says, "Open my eyes that I may see!" Now, I needed to learn how to grow in this gift. There were some new age practices in massage school, such as yoga and energy work. I opted out of this class with another guy who was from a Pentecostal family. I pulled out the good things from the school and let go of the other things that were not of God.

During this time, Vicki sold her house. We needed a place to live. Jurgen's boss told us about a little house that was for rent. It was small, but we knew we could fix it up and make it our own. That is exactly what we did. We called our new place the "Love Shack." It cost $250 a month. Jurgen made it look nice.

He painted the whole inside. We bought some used furniture to match. It wasn't a beautiful or fancy place, but it was ours. We were excited to have that little place to call our own. We didn't need much. We were sober and walking with the Lord. We were happy.

We had good memories in the "Love Shack." My parents came to visit, and Jurgen's mother and sister came to visit. I am not sure what my parents thought of our new faith in Jesus. I knew they were worried about me and my former lifestyle. I believed they were happy and relieved that I was no longer doing drugs or drinking. We took them to our new church, and they enjoyed it. Little did we know that we would not stay there too long. The Lord was going to move us.

My aunt, Janis, who prayed for me at the reunion, worked for Pat Robertson for a season. He had a Christian talk show called the 700 Club. She worked as a prayer warrior. People would call in for prayer requests, and she would answer the calls. From time to time, I would turn on that show and see her face. It would make me cry. I was so drawn to my Christian family in Georgia. I felt like we were supposed to be with them. My cousin Heidi said that she had an extra room in her house that we could stay in if we ever decided to move to Georgia.

I told Jurgen that I thought we were to move to the Atlanta area where our family was and to be a part of Atlanta City Church. Jurgen talked to our pastor. Because both Jurgen and I were bringing many people to church, my pastor did not feel it was the right timing. This was a great lesson for me. Very often, I will get direction from the Lord or insight ahead of time. This is where I have had to learn to wait patiently for His timing. Timing is everything.

I finally got baptized by Pastor Pat in the nearby swimming pool and was finishing up massage school. The day I was baptized, a lady from my massage school came over to my home to tutor me for our upcoming anatomy test. In return, I was going to put her on an exercise program. When she arrived, I saw a large tattoo on her arm. My spiritual eyes were open, and I was curious.

I asked her what the tattoo was, and she told me she was a witch. This was the same day I was baptized, and now there was a witch in my house. I tried not to show my concern. I asked her if she was a good witch or a bad witch. She said she was a good witch and involved in Wicca. I know now that I was in spiritual warfare training 101 right off the bat.

I was frightened because I was a baby Christian and still learning about spiritual things. Jurgen and I called our pastor. He was kind enough to come over and talk to us about spiritual warfare and to remove any fears we may have had. He told us that we had the resurrection power of Christ in us and that we did not need to be afraid of the dark side.

We were warriors for the Lord, and we were in boot camp. God loves all people, and so do I. The Bible says that our battle is not against people. We are in a spiritual battle. Ephesians 6:12 says, "For we wrestle not against flesh and blood, but against principalities, against powers, against the rulers of the darkness of the world, against spiritual wickedness in the high places." We were learning.

I took the anatomy test. In the past, I felt I had to cheat to succeed. I believed a lie that I was not smart enough to pass. It was as if there were a fog over my mind. After giving my life to Jesus, I was aware that it was not an option to cheat. I now had a conscience and integrity. I received an "A" on that anatomy test in massage school. God had been so merciful to me. I did not want to grieve Him. I had to do the work and trust God. This was all a new way of life.

Well, guess what? I got a 4.0 average and graduated with honors. That is a testament to trusting God. I learned, and am still learning, that when God has called you to do something, He will get you through.

As massage school was winding down, we were offered a class to help us discover what we wanted to do with our massage skills. One of my friends in my school was the sister of Joe Perry, who is the famous guitar player in the band Arrow Smith. She said she desired to travel with the band and massage the rock stars. I said, "I think I am called to massage the church ladies." That is quite a contrast.

38

GRADUATING FROM MASSAGE SCHOOL/ MOVING TO ATLANTA

After graduating from massage school, our pastor and Jurgen both felt like it was time for us to move to Atlanta to be with our extended family. I called my cousin, Heidi, and her husband, Alan, in Georgia and let them know that we were on our way. They had a room just for us in their home. They were elated that we were coming to live with them.

Heidi and Alan Winter and their family were a missionary family with a gift of hospitality. They had a big house, and they loved having people around. The more, the merrier was their motto. We would fit right in and not miss a beat.

Pastor Pat and his wife, Cindy, and the whole church sent us out with a blessing. They gave us gifts and prayed over us in a powerful way. One of the girls who prayed for us said she felt that we were going to go where God was moving. She sensed we were going to be trained up to be a part of the end-time revival. Wow! I was ready for this new adventure. We both were. It was the timing of the Lord, and we knew it.

Jurgen traded in his work truck for a used truck he had bought from a friend. We also bought an old used car. I have strong memories of the day we left Tucson for Georgia. We drove in Jurgen's old truck and hooked the used car behind it. We put all our belongings in the bed of the truck.

We left very early in the morning. Our pastor and friends were there to send us off. As I looked into the rearview mirror, I could see them waving. They were getting smaller and smaller as our future and the new season was getting closer and closer.

I had changed so much in a short amount of time. I took out my hair weave, went back to my natural color, and completely changed how I dressed. I did not need or desire unhealthy attention. In fact, I went in the opposite direction, fully covered myself, and did not want any attention at all. Eventually, the pendulum that was swinging from one extreme to the other with my hair and the way I dressed began to balance out.

Moving from Tucson to Georgia was a type of symbolism of leaving my old life and entering a new life. The extreme changes were both spiritual and natural. We did not have a lot of material things. We had each other and God. We were ready for a new chapter in our lives.

It took us about three days to travel across the country from Tucson to Georgia. I was in intense prayer most of the time. I did not know what the prayer was about. I did, however, find out a short while after our arrival.

We landed in south Atlanta, Fairburn, Georgia, in January 1997. The Lord knew it would be a safe place to grow and get planted spiritually. He knew it was the right place to start a family and to build a business, along with growing and serving in ministry.

Heidi and Alan had a beautiful three-story home with lots of land and a lake. Through the years, I have seen many people baptized in that lake. They had three children who were in school at the time. When we drove to their home, the children had made welcome signs for us. We really felt loved and accepted. It was much like the Walton's home from the 70's television series, *The Waltons*.

As we got settled, Jurgen started to build his painting business. He learned his skills from his father in Germany, who was a master painter. Jurgen had the talent and experience. Now, he needed to build a team and a client base. I got a job at a chiropractor's office doing massage therapy.

Alan and Heidi were youth pastors and elders at Atlanta City Church. They also had a passion for missions. I believe that is why I was in deep prayer on the trip to Georgia. Not long after we got to their home, they took a leap of faith into full-time mission work. Meanwhile, Jurgen and I were immediately dunked into full-time ministry with them. We fit right in.

Our church had about six hundred people attending from all walks of life and every skin color and ethnicity. It was a non-denominational church. They believed in the full gospel; this included the gifts of the spirit. The worship was always lively, and I looked forward to church every week.

39

ATLANTA CITY CHURCH AND THREE-WEEK MISSION TRIP

Jurgen and I were in an accelerated spiritual boot camp. We were learning fast and growing. Our pastor at the time was a gifted teacher of the Word of God. We were blessed to have him teach us for many years. He was passionate about teaching. This is where we got to learn about the Scriptures and how to apply them in our lives. That was crucial. We were building a strong spiritual foundation while building our new lives.

Not long after our arrival, Alan and Heidi were preparing to put on a large youth retreat in Tennessee. We were excited to help them in any way we could. They put us to work. It was great to serve alongside them.

Jurgen and I flourished and met many wonderful people. The youth retreat was exhausting but powerful. Working with my family and among the leadership for this retreat was rewarding. I had about thirteen family members in the church. There were three first cousins at the time, all of whom were in leadership, and their children.

About six months after the youth retreat, Alan and Heidi were preparing for a large three-week mission trip to Guyana and Brazil. The mission group they started was called "Frontline Missions." There were forty of us going together from our church. This mission trip turned out to be one of the most memorable experiences of my life, not just for me but for so many.

Frontline Missions Brazil Missions Trip - 1997

The purpose of this trip was to bring the gospel of Jesus to the sick, orphans, and those who were lost. We also supported the local churches to which Frontline Missions were connected. We brought a worship team, mime team, medical team, a prayer team, and pastors and others who preached. Taking forty people on a mission trip to two other countries was no easy task.

Jurgen and I were able to learn so many wonderful things from Alan and Heidi about preparing for ministry. The good, bad, and ugly. Ministry is not always glamorous; it is hard work. But so very worth it.

I found my position on the team as an intercessor. This is another word for prayer warrior. I was privileged to pray for many and lead them to Christ. The Scripture that comes to me is Mark 16:15, "Jesus said to them, 'Go into all the world and preach the gospel to all creation.'" That is exactly what we were doing.

I found myself crying a lot. I felt the heart of God for His people as I was learning how to walk with Him. I felt His heart while holding

Frontline Missions Guyana Missions Trip - 1997

little children in the orphanage in Guyana. I also felt this while helping sick people who lived in tree houses in the Brazilian jungle.

I was weeping. I felt like the weeping prophet Jeremiah. I saw this Scripture and realized I was weeping for a reason. It was a form of prayer. Psalm 126:5 says, "Those who sow in tears will reap with songs of joy."

I was in a season of learning how to carry God's heart and discovering what my gifts were and how to use them. Meanwhile, our team had to travel from Guyana to Brazil. The women and teenagers went by small plane, and the men and a couple of women traveled in the back of an old English army truck through the Brazilian jungle. Jurgen was on that truck. He said it was an unforgettable ride. He saw colorful parrots, jaguars, and much more.

My friend, Peggy, from Tucson, flew out to be with us on this trip. All the people who went on this trip have a special bond that remains to this day. When we arrived home, I was so appreciative of everything we had. We had a big bed and lots of running water for our shower. After seeing all the poverty and children playing in the sewers, I felt much more appreciative of all the little things.

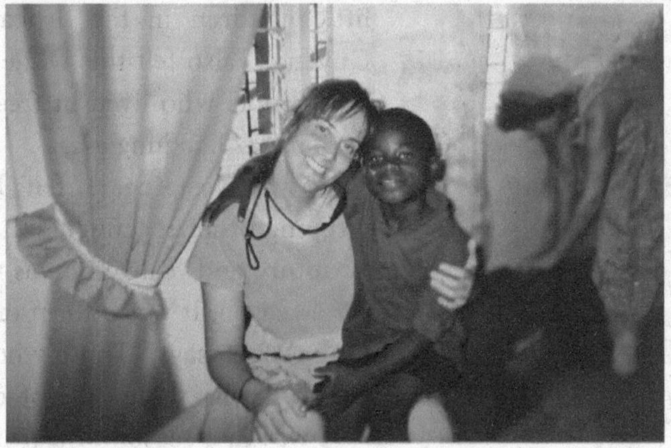

Guyana Orphanage - 1997

I believe I have four major seasons in my life.

One, growing up and following my own path.

Two, giving my life to Jesus.

Three, coming into an intense learning season and putting into practice what I was learning.

And four, giving away and teaching what I had learned.

Coming to Georgia and being a part of Atlanta City Church was an accelerated learning season. It was fast and furious. Jurgen and I loved every minute of it. We did it together.

Jurgen and I were on a journey discovering our purpose and giftings and calling unto the Lord. Not just individually but together as a team. The church was a great place to serve in many different ministries and discover what we were called to do. We used to be bodybuilders together. Now, we are training to be church bodybuilders—helping to build the Body of Christ.

Here are a few of the ministries that we were honored to serve and grow in: youth ministry, intercession team, alter team, dance team, financial classes, prophetic classes, and Bible studies. We also took and taught marriage ministry classes and were a part of outreach to the homeless. Jurgen played guitar and was on the worship team for a while.

In this season, I was learning how to know God intimately and not just do things for Him. I aggressively learned all I could. I was a part of many women's conferences. I'd travel to places where people who were preaching and teaching walked in the power of God. I was hungry for more of Him. I had tasted and seen that the Lord is good. I could not get enough.

40

BROWNSVILLE REVIVAL IN PENSACOLA

I had heard about a real revival going on in Pensacola, Florida. Many people in the body of Christ were talking about it. It was 1997 when I first visited. This was a real outpouring of the presence of God. Brownsville Assembly of God Church had been praying for a move of God for some time. The pastor was John Kilpatrick. He had invited an evangelist named Steve Hill to preach. They both had a real hunger for God and a love for His people.

The revival started in 1995 and went on for about six years. There were approximately 5,500 people attending each night. It was estimated that more than two and a half million people attended. I spent much time at the revival and returned many times until my last visit in 2000. I cannot describe how beautiful this revival was and how much it changed me.

We had a van at the time, and I would repeatedly drive bunches of people down to the revival. We named my van "The Glory Van." Sometimes, I would go to help someone get free, or I would just go to get in the river of God. We would stay at hotels or host homes. The people of Brownsville church would open their homes for guests to stay.

I knew that the gift of prayer that was activated and operating in my life was unique. At the Brownsville revival, I saw other people praying like me. They prayed with great compassion, travail, tears, groanings, etc. It was very encouraging. I was honored to take part in their corporate intercession meeting. I saw men and women of all ages crying out to God for souls. I was learning and growing quickly.

One of my favorite parts of the revival was listening to Steve Hill's powerful message. He always released a pure, powerful, and convicting message. I got to see the results of prayer and the message colliding. Hundreds, if not thousands of people, came to the altar to repent and get close to God. This was not a manipulation of man. This was the power and presence of Almighty God. He was drawing His people to Himself.

I was forever changed by experiencing this revival. I could never go back to a normal, powerless Christian life. Nor did I want to. I discovered that revival starts in our own hearts. It is wonderful to also experience it corporately. I believe the presence of God and the fear of the Lord that I received at this revival have sustained me through life's valleys and mountaintops.

41

TORONTO AIRPORT VINEYARD REVIVAL

Another wonderful corporate move of God I experienced that was life-changing was the Toronto Revival. It started as the Toronto Airport Vineyard Church. They changed the name to the "Toronto Blessing." It became the center of a global revival. The revival started around 1994.

Before the revival started, John and Carol Arnott, who are the pastors of the Toronto Blessing, were spiritually and emotionally tired and were burning out. They were seeking God with all their heart and spending a lot of time in prayer. They heard about a revival in Argentina, which was led by a man named Carlos Annacondia. They went to the Argentinian revival and were powerfully touched by God. They came away refreshed.

They hoped they could bring that back to their church. That is exactly what happened. There were 120 people in a meeting at their church one night in 1994. They asked a man named Randy Clark to come speak. He was also seeking God in a powerful way.

God showed up in a way they did not expect. It had not occurred to them that God would throw a massive party where people would laugh and roll as they cried. People became so empowered by the presence of God that emotional hurts from childhood just lifted off. Some people were overcome physically by God's power. They had to be carried out.

The first time I went to the Toronto Blessing was with Jurgen. I got prayed for and fell out under the power of God and began laughing so hard. It was not a funny, "Ha, ha, ha," laugh, as one does when one momentarily laughs at something. Instead, it was a deep, supernatural laughter filled with joy. The kind of joy that is from the presence of God.

The Scripture says, Psalm 16:11: "You make known to me the path of life, in Your presence there is fullness of joy; at Your right hand are pleasures forever more."

Jurgen had a harder time yielding to the Lord. He was not sure about all of it, but he was there to cover me. I recall lying on the floor under the beautiful presence of the Lord. I happened to be in an area on the floor of the church with about three or four Japanese folks who were also laughing hysterically under the power of God. It was as if we were all connected to this river of joy that was so powerful it was electric. The Lord would touch us. We would all laugh hard, and then it would stop. We'd all be quiet. Then, another wave of laughter would hit. This went on for what seemed like hours.

Jurgen waited patiently until God finished what he was doing. When I got up, my stomach muscles hurt so bad from laughing. I was not the same. Something had changed. I was lighter and freer. The Bible talks about the joy of the Lord being our strength. Joy is a weapon, and it is very important.

A lot of the emphasis of the Toronto Blessing was the joy and the refreshing of the saints of God who were doing His work. I am still, to this day, powerfully impacted by the impartation, refreshment, and supernatural joy I received. There were also many other reports that came from this revival. Reports of new boldness, conversions, trans-formed lives, and demonic strongholds broken.

Even to this day, the Holy Spirit will sometimes give me an impartation of joy that seemingly comes out of the blue. I know how to yield to His presence and not resist. He fills me with His supernatural joy to overcome heaviness during spiritual warfare.

Or He may do it to help me assist a client the next day who is struggling with depression. You cannot give out what you don't have. I am grateful that I had the opportunity to visit these outpourings to get these impartations.

42

SUPERNATURAL POWER OF GOD ENCOUNTERS! RUTH HEFLIN/ENCOUNTER WITH GLORY

Christianity is uncompromisingly supernatural. If we take away the supernatural, we take away Christianity. Jesus Christ was born of a virgin. That is supernatural. He rose from the dead. His resurrection is supernatural. This resurrection power of Jesus Christ lives within us through the Holy Spirit. The Holy Spirit helps us to supernaturally walk out our faith.

I was so tired of trying to do things on my own and in my own strength. When I began experiencing His power to transform me, it was such a relief. This is why I was so drawn to the revivals and people who operated in power. The false Jesus of human works was not interesting to me. Once I tasted and saw the goodness of God and his supernatural power, it was life-changing.

Many people are drawn to the supernatural. A lot of them look in the wrong places and receive counterfeit power from the wrong source—from the dark side. There is renewed interest in the supernatural. Unfortunately, a lot of this is interested in the occult or the dark side. We must be vigilant to make sure our understanding of the supernatural is informed by the Bible and not paganism.

One powerful woman of God who operated in the supernatural was Ruth Ward Heflin. She was a Christian minister among the nations for nearly 40 years. In 1997, she returned to the United States to help with the American revival. She was known for her prophetic anointing, revelation, ability to teach, and leading people into spontaneous worship.

Ruth Heflin and Sister Silvana in 1999

Ruth ministered to heads of state and leaders throughout the world. She was the director of Calvary Pentecostal Campground in Ashland, Virginia, as well as an international prayer ministry in Jerusalem. She wrote many books.

I have read and own most of them. Her bestselling books were "Glory," "Revival Glory," "River Glory," "Harvest Glory," "Golden Glory," "Unifying Glory," and "Revelation Glory." These books are being used worldwide as handbooks for revival.

We were going to the same church as my aunt Janis. She was so full of the Lord and wisdom. She knew we were trying to have children and that we were having a hard time. She wanted to take a trip to Ruth Heflin's Camp meeting. She invited Jurgen and I to go with her. We accepted her invitation with great expectation and excitement. We were going to seek God and pray to conceive children.

What a wonderful time we had. It was about an eight-hour drive, but it was beautiful scenery. We talked about the goodness of God and prayed and worshiped the whole trip. The camp meeting did not disappoint. We felt the presence of God and His glory as soon as we drove onto the property. There was preaching, teaching, worship, and prayer. We listened to a message from a couple from South Africa. They were part of Ruth's team. So, we trusted them.

We felt led to ask them to pray for us to have children. To our surprise, they said they were gifted to pray for people who had difficulty getting pregnant. Bingo! We were at the right place at the right time.

The couple and their team prayed for us. I fell out under the power of God. I heard them circling Jurgen and I as they prayed. They began to prophesy over us. They said, "We see a baby! Oh, we see another baby." They also said they saw money coming down from heaven. I believed that represented provision related to the children.

Do you know that we went home from Ruth Heflin's camp meeting and immediately got pregnant? Don't give up on your dreams. Sometimes, you must press in, get desperate, and fight as the Lord leads. The Bible says in Matthew 11:12, "And from the days of John the Baptist until now, the kingdom of heaven suffers violence and the violent take it by force."

The prayer team had broken a curse off my womb. I believe the curse had come when I aborted my child years prior to this camp meeting. Now that I was serving Jesus, I had the power to break curses from my past. The Bible says, "Submit to God, resist the devil and he will flee" (James 4:7). We must do our part.

I knew God was real, and so was the Bible. I wanted to see the Bible come alive. I was delighted at Ruth Heflin's camp meeting to see God's power in action. I also saw a sign and a wonder. The Bible says in Acts 8:13, "Even Simon himself believed, and after being baptized he continued with Philip. And seeing signs and great miracles performed, he was amazed."

While at Ruth's camp meeting, she showed us all a video on a big screen. It was a video of a woman named Silvania from Brazil. She was dying of four types of cancer in her organs. Her body was beginning to stink because of her illness. People did not want to be around her. The exception was a small church in her village. The church prayed for her and did not give up.

One morning, her little church went to visit her. They were amazed that God had healed her and given her brand-new organs. In this process of healing, oil began to flow supernaturally from her body. Later, gold dust began to be manifested on her face and the crown of her head. As she praised and worshiped, this phenomenon of gold dust and oil would show up. Her pastor gathered the gold flakes and mixed them with olive oil in a bottle to be used to anoint the sick and needy.

I trusted Ruth and her discernment. She felt this was the Lord's doing. She even flew out to Brazil to see Silvania. Ruth saw firsthand the oil and gold dust that was produced in Silvania. She brought some of it back with her to her own camp meeting. She also brought back a video that showed the miracle of oil and gold dust as it happened. I was intrigued as I watched it.

I was not afraid when Ruth asked if she could pray for us using the miracle oil. I did feel the presence of God. I was very aware of not just opening myself up to anything. I knew I must test the spirits, but I felt peace.

I told the Lord that if this were real, I would like to see Silvania in person. Nine months later, I was very pregnant with my first daughter, Heidi, in Georgia when I got a phone call from a friend. She said,

"Did you know that Ruth Heflin is speaking at a church in our area with the lady from Brazil?" Wow, I knew I had to go.

When I arrived at the little church in Georgia, I could feel the weighty presence of the Lord. I could feel Him even in the parking lot. When I stepped into the church, I saw that it was full of people who were spiritually curious. I saw Ruth up front with Silvania about to share her testimony with an interpreter because Silvania spoke Portuguese.

As she finished sharing her testimony about how God healed her body, the worship began. This is when I saw firsthand the gold dust coming from her head and the oil in her hand. She asked if people wanted to come up and stand in line for prayer.

I and many others immediately got up. I waddled to the front because I was so pregnant. I was amazed as I watched the gold dust come out of her head. God's presence was so strong. She came to me, lifted my shirt, and said, "Baby?" I said, "Yes, baby." It's the same word in both Portuguese and English.

She put gold dust and oil from heaven all over my pregnant belly and prayed for me. Oh, what a joy. I fell to the floor under the glorious presence of the Lord to rest and soak it all in. I must have looked like a beached whale with my belly sticking straight up in the air. I didn't care. It was a wonderful experience. I carried my Bible around for years with the gold dust in the pages from that night.

Some would say, "Why would God do something like that?" Well, for me, He can do whatever He wants. It was a token of His love for me. I had asked God if I could see it firsthand, and He allowed me to see it. I saw another side to Him. The Bible says to come to Him with childlike faith.

I believe these wonderful experiences have given me great faith to abide in Him and stay steady in my walk with Him even when I don't feel or see Him. I have had a lot of supernatural healing and experiences along my journey. I believe it is partly because I was seeking Him with great anticipation and expectation. I believe He is drawn to that kind of faith.

43

DREAMS AND VISION/HEALING
OF MY WOMB AND STUTTERING

The Lord has gifted me with dreams and visions. I have about twenty-five dream journals full of recorded dreams and visions that the Lord has given me. Often, He shares with me what is going on in my heart or about what is happening in my life. I get warnings in my dreams or information about what is happening to other people. This is for me to partner in prayer with the Lord to bring change to a situation.

I am grateful for this gift and have given a lot of time and energy to stewarding it well. I hope to write a book or at least a training manual about dreams and what to do with them. Sometimes, I would have an open vision. These are from the Lord when I am awake. One day, I was with Jurgen in the grocery store. This was a few years after I had given my life to the Lord.

We were shopping in the vegetable aisle. Suddenly, I saw a large vision of me speaking on stage in front of a large group of women. Jurgen started asking me a question, and I told him to be quiet because I was having an open vision. He responded, "Here in the grocery store?" I said, "Yes."

When the vision was over, I told God that I thought that would be exciting and I would be obedient to whatever He wanted me to do.

But I asked Him, "What about my stuttering?" I had a chronic stutter for over thirty years. I asked Him to heal me.

It was not overnight when He answered my prayer. It was in God's timing. Jurgen and I were invited to serve at another youth retreat. We were happy to do it. We loved ministering to the youth and serving leaders. One night during the conference, we had a wonderful worship time. I was in the back, minding my own business and serving.

A speaker named Jude Fouquier came out. He paused for a moment. Then he said that God would not let him go on with his message until he released a word of knowledge that he received from God. He said that his wife was a stutterer and God had healed her. He spoke out, "Someone in this room is a stutterer, and God is healing you."

At that moment, I knew it was me, and so did a lot of the people around me who knew me. I felt as if I stepped into another realm. It was as if a fireball or heat hit my mouth and loosened my jaw. The fire was doing something in my mouth and tongue, like rearranging it. I was crying at the same time because of God's healing presence.

My friends and family members who were at the retreat knew I stuttered. They gathered around me and prayed for me. They were crying, too. It was beautiful. The enemy wanted to take my voice. God wanted me to speak for Him. After this encounter, I talked differently because God's anointing was still on my mouth.

I went home and learned to talk a different way. One thing I did realize was that when I stayed filled up in God's presence, I would not stutter. When I was tired and empty, I would start to stutter again. When I stuttered, this was a sign for me to pull back into my prayer closet and spend time with Him.

I have had many wonderful opportunities to speak in front of people, churches, and groups. When I shared my testimony or spoke as a keynote speaker, the Lord would touch my mouth and rearrange it like He did that day. My husband would be so shocked at how I would speak. He said that when I spoke, it was smooth as silk. Even I was amazed.

44

TAKES A VILLAGE/GRATEFUL FOR MENTOR

The Lord's hand was on my life in a tangible way. He was redeeming what the enemy had stolen. It was a process of walking it out.

I am grateful for the many mentors, pastors, spiritual mothers and fathers, and friends and family that God placed in my life to help me grow. One of them was Bonnie. She was a mentor and spiritual mother to me. She fought for me and helped me grow.

One way she helped me grow was with my children. My children were one of the most difficult but rewarding gifts the Lord had given me. There was a battle over me to be a good mother.

I could not see past the lies that it was possible or likely that someone with my background of abortions, addictions, and a deep sense of rejection from my father could translate into me becoming a good mother.

Living in the world, the enemy tried to put death in my womb. Now, the Lord was bringing life to my womb and was helping me to be the mother He had called me to be. I learned that I was born to give birth naturally and spiritually.

Another way Bonnie helped me was by walking me through the process of getting my life story written. She and I would go away to write with the Lord. Once we went to a beach house to write. Another time, we went to a cabin in the mountains. We went to get away from distractions, to seek the Lord, and to write my testimony.

Part of the writing process was she'd help me through the deception and lies I believed. It was a therapeutic process of discovery. It was like being counseled as I wrote. She was a pivotal part of my growth.

45

CURSE IS REVERSED: FIRST MIRACLE BABY!

In 1999, I was thirty-six years old and pregnant with my first child, Heidi. I knew having a baby was a gift. Jurgen and I lived in the basement apartment of my cousin Heidi's home. It was perfect for our first child. The pregnancy was a wonderful experience for me. I was delighted to have a baby growing inside of me.

I was pregnant at the same time with another girl at our church who was seventeen. The two pregnancies were so different. She was not planning on having a baby. She was still in high school. I had already seen the world and had so many experiences, good and bad. I had lived a lot of life; therefore, I was grateful to be pregnant. I didn't feel like I was missing anything. She, on the other hand, resented that she had gotten pregnant so young and had not experienced college or life. It was two very different scenarios.

In May of 1999, I was close to delivering Heidi. Jurgen and I were settled and in a good place spiritually and physically. I had wonderful support from my church.

The church ladies gave me a baby shower. Forty-five women attended. I was overwhelmed by the outpouring of love and gifts. I felt God's love through these ladies. I got everything I would ever need for my child. In my thirty-six years, I had never experienced the love of a community like this. It was powerful. I felt the faithfulness of God.

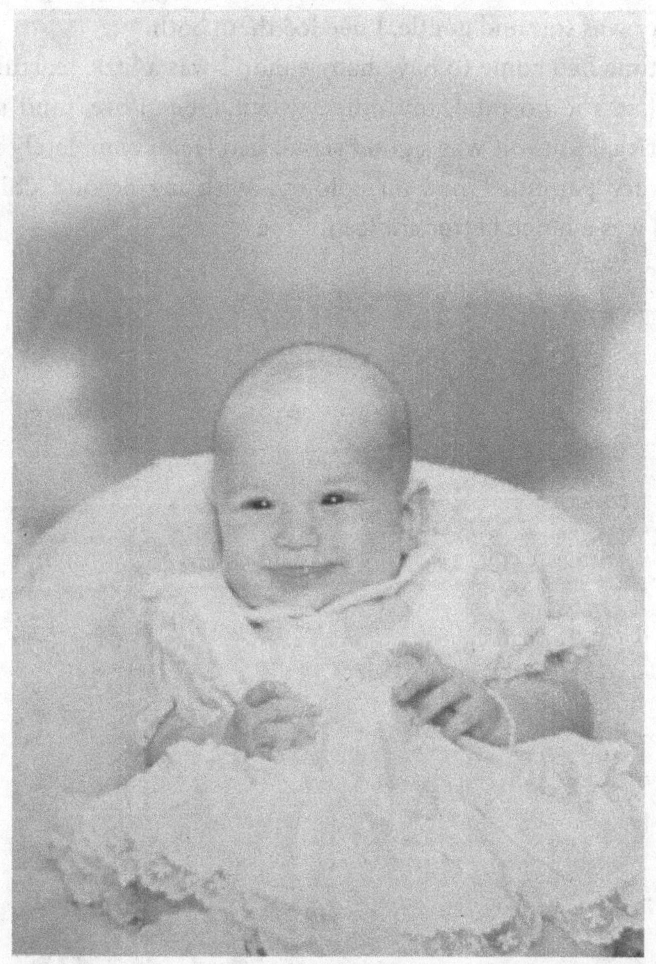

Baby Heidi-Lynn - 1999

The doctor told me that my pregnancy was high-risk because of my age. So, Jurgen and I drove monthly to downtown Atlanta to get a pregnancy checkup. We used these times to go on dates, explore Atlanta, and draw closer to one another. It was a remarkable experience. I had lived thirty-six years on my own. Now everything was going to totally change.

I asked two of my cousins to be in the room with me and Jurgen during delivery. Both of my cousins were experienced in helping with childbirth. One cousin had a strong, somewhat aggressive personality. The other was soft and gentle. I needed them both.

The time had come to have baby Heidi. I was a little fearful. When we went to the hospital, my nurse was named "Love," and she was from Africa. I knew it was a good sign. I had Heidi completely natural. It was very painful. I had an epidural with my second child. The epidural was a much better choice for me.

Heidi Lynn Hornemann

I remember vividly when it was time to bring baby Heidi home. The nurse wheeled me out in a wheelchair with baby Heidi in my arms. I sat in the wheelchair outside the hospital when Jurgen went to the parking garage to get the car. As I was holding my new baby, many thoughts went through my mind. I had seen a lot of darkness in the world. I wanted to protect my baby. I thought, "Oh God, it is such a crazy world out there. Please keep my baby safe."

I WAS A PERFORMANCE-ORIENTED CHILD GROWING UP. THAT CAME through in my parenting. I wanted to be a perfect mother and protect my child from the things I had gone through. When I brought Heidi home, our whole life changed—and it was not just for the good.

My mother came to see baby Heidi and helped us for ten days. This was helpful. I cried when she left. I was worn out. Jurgen said that I had changed since having Heidi. It was not for the better. I felt the responsibility for this baby, and I was carrying the weight of that. I ultimately ended up in post-partum depression, chronic fatigue, and fibromyalgia.

I was on fire for Jesus. I was a born-again believer who was Spirit-filled. How could I be depressed? We are human and have a soul to deal with. The soul is the mind, will, and emotions. I was still growing and walking my life out with Christ. It is not a microwave life with Jesus. It is more like a crock pot. Some things require patience and time. I needed more deliverance, and I was not going to give up.

It was a depressingly dark time. Yet I loved being a mother. I have such compassion for people who suffer from depression. I needed to keep fighting. I needed to get to the root issue. I heard about a doctor who understood how to get to the root of the issues.

I didn't want to go on a bunch of drugs. I'd been on drugs in my former life, and I didn't want that. This doctor was kind and gave me hope. He gave me light prescriptions for an antidepressant and something to help me sleep. He told me to keep going after my emotional and spiritual healing.

The mild drugs helped me until I could get free. I was aggressive and persistent in getting my healing. Little by little, the lies were pulled out of me, and the truth was being deposited. I remember a friend from church told me, "You don't have to be a perfect mother. All she needs is your love. God gave you this child, and you are the perfect mother for her."

I WAS IN THE FRONT OF EVERY HEALING LINE AT OUR CHURCH. I HAD many people praying for me. I journaled my experiences because I knew someday, I would help people who were suffering and would give them hope. There was purpose in the pain, and that kept me going.

One year later, I heard the Lord say, "You are ready to go off the medicine." I was fearful. I did not want to go back into that dark place. I pressed past the fear to obey the Lord. I came off the medicine, and I have been free from depression ever since.

It is not as if the heaviness and depression do not try to come back. I now have tools to push them back and keep them off me. Whatever you're going through, don't give up.

46

A CALL OF INTIMACY WITH THE LORD AND TO BIRTH MINISTRIES

Everyone has different callings and giftings. It was obvious that God was using my gift of prayer to start or birth ministries. This ministry is like a spiritual midwife. I was learning what that meant and was gaining wisdom through experience. The scripture I found to describe that type of travailing or birthing prayer. Gal. 4:19: "My little children, for whom I travail in birth again until Christ be formed in you." This is Paul giving expression to his prayer for the Galatians. Note that Paul is "travailing" again. Those to whom he is writing are already Christians.

OUTREACH MINISTRY TO STRIP CLUBS WITH VICTORIA'S FRIENDS

In the year 2000, I got a phone call from two mighty women of God who were in the beginning stages of their ministries. They were both starting ministries to help women who were victims of sexual exploitation. They wanted to give them access to transformative care.

One of them was Victoria. She started *Victoria's Friends,* which is an outreach program for the strip clubs of Atlanta. It is a non-profit organization that provides support, physical restoration, training, and equipping women working in the sex industry. Their mission is to individually serve women who are lost, trapped, and in need of support.

The other woman was Mary, who started the ministry *Wellspring Living*. Mary wanted to build a safe house for the women to get healed. Mary's church and home were near my home.

Victoria lived about one hour north of me. Someone had told them about Jurgen and I and our testimony. They wanted to meet me and discuss their vision. The three of us met and spent hours talking and praying about what God wanted to do. At this meeting, I learned more about their passion and their ministries, and how I could help.

Victoria shared her story with us. She had worked in the strip clubs of Atlanta for many years. She hit rock bottom from drug and alcohol abuse, as well as prostitution. In 1990, she began following Jesus. She got married to her husband, Jeff. She then began *Victoria's Friends* ministry in 2000.

This ministry brought "Baskets of Love" to the women working in the strip clubs. Each basket contained beautiful things for the women. The baskets also had information on a hotline connected to the ministry. The hotline was there just in case someone was in immediate trouble and needed intervention.

Victoria's Friends raised up teams that delivered the baskets to the dressing rooms of the local strip clubs. The outreach offered a glimmer of hope to those who were ready to leave but who may have doubted that they had support for making such a move.

Mary, however, had a vision of a home for girls coming out of strip clubs, sexual abuse, or bondage. With the help of the church and the community, she started the *Home of Redeeming Love* as a supporting ministry under *Wellspring Living*.

The home was located close to mine. So, this made it ideal for me to spend a lot of time there. It was a beautiful home that had many rooms for the women to live and Wellspring program was a one-year program of teaching and training. Its purpose was to get the women back on their feet and in all-around health.

I had the pleasure of partnering in prayer with Mary for the start of this ministry. I was able to build relationships with the girls. I got to share my testimony, pray for them, and encourage them as they grew. At one point, we had a girl from the Wellspring program stay in our home for three months.

LEADERS OF RESCUE MISSION

47

LEADERS OF RESCUE MISSION IN STRIP CLUBS

ictoria and her husband met with Jurgen and I. They asked if we would lead the outreach teams into the strip clubs. Wow, this was down our alley. We had come out of this lifestyle. We had a great understanding of it. Now, we had a chance to go back in and help those who were hurting, suicidal, hopeless, addicted, and helpless.

As Christians, we are all called to be God's hands and feet in this world. Not all are called to do outreach into the strip clubs of Atlanta. We knew without a doubt that we were called. We accepted the offer. We had no idea what a growing and life-changing experience this would be. We were in training to be leaders, not just for then but for the future.

As leaders of Victoria's Friends outreach, the Lord was teaching and leading us. We trained teams to go into the strip clubs to minister to the girls. We also had a prayer team that prayed for us before and after the outreach. Jurgen and I were learning the good, bad, and the ugly about becoming leaders. We were on the fast track of learning spiritual warfare.

The Lord dunked us into the battle zone. We were in the deep end spiritually, and we had better learn how to fight. The strip clubs are the devil's territory and playground. The battle was fierce, but we knew we were called. I look back and see all that the Lord did in that season. We would not be who we are today if not for that training. We are grateful for that.

We learned to humble ourselves, to forgive quickly, and to lead people who did not want to be led. We also learned to work with the community and be covered by a pastor and a church body. We found out in a deeper way that God loves to move outside the church and into the dark places. That is where his light shines most.

We led *Victoria's Friends* outreaches for about six or seven years. We learned to rely on prayer and the Holy Spirit to lead, guide, and cover us. We trained our teams to be united and to walk in love, not judgment. We found that the key was to build relationships with those we were trying to reach. We built relationships with the bouncers, owners of the Clubs, and the house moms.

House moms are hired to take care of the women in the back dressing room. They make the schedules, help with wardrobe, and make sure the women do not go onstage intoxicated. Many house moms really care about the women. That is how we got a lot of our openings.

Jurgen and I, along with our teams, got to build relationships, and we knew the names of many of the women who worked in the clubs. We also knew the names of many prostitutes, drug addicts, homeless people, bouncers, gangsters, and owners of bars.

If you want to get into the heart of a woman, ask her about her children. Many (not all) of the women worked in the clubs to support their children because their husbands abused or abandoned them. They would open their hearts to us and tell us their story. I could write a book on the many miraculous events we experienced during our outreaches into the Atlanta strip clubs.

We listened to their heartbreaking stories. We loved them, hugged them, and gave them beautiful baskets. After years of building relationships and saturating the outreach with prayer, we began to see God moving in amazing ways.

We would give the girls baby showers and birthday parties. We went to funerals when a girl would pass away. We had a place down-town for them to come get prayer for practical needs. We also began to make baskets for their children. That really touched them.

We always met before an outreach and prayed over the baskets. Then, after the outreach, we would go out to eat and do a debriefing. This is the time the team members could share what they experienced.

Most of the time, the girls on our outreach team would bring their husbands. Jurgen and the husbands would drive us and stay in the parking lot. They would give out bouncer bags to the bouncers and would talk to them outside in the parking lot. We got permission to go into the strip clubs from the owners or the house-moms. It was always God opening the door. We would never push our way in. God would always protect and cover us.

We were scattering seeds of the word of God and of love. I remember the Lord breaking my heart for these women in my prayer time. I could feel His heart for them. I cried and wailed until I could not cry anymore. When I went into the clubs that night, the girls felt the presence of God in me and His love. Every time I hugged a girl, they cried. I allowed the Lord to move through me. It was such an honor. We are just His vessels.

I only stayed with *Wellspring Living* for about four years. Well-spring ended up with a very impactful ministry helping the victims of sex trafficking.

48

9/11

In 2001, we lived in the basement apartment in Georgia with our daughter, who was now two years old. I remember clearly September 11th. I finished changing my daughter's diaper when I turned to look at the television. I could not believe what I was seeing. New York City was under attack.

I recall seeing the planes fly into the World Trade Center. Many thoughts came to my mind. In 1980, my parents took me to New York City. We ate at the top of the World Trade Center at a restaurant called *Windows on the World*. I'd never seen a view like that. We were up so high. We looked down at the Statue of Liberty. The cars below us looked like the size of matchboxes.

Now, it was almost twenty years later. The same Twin Towers that my parents took me to were now on fire and falling. I had a quick flashback of a prophetic warning dream the Lord gave me seven months earlier. I didn't know exactly what it meant until I saw the towers.

The dream was full of symbolism. In the dream, I saw a large field where people were eating, drinking, and enjoying life. I saw a mountain and two trains going around the mountain. The trains collided in a terrible crash. Cows went flying in the air from the mountain.

(Cows mean prosperity in biblical symbolism.) The people were in shock.

Then, President Bush and the army stepped in. This is when I woke up with the hairs on my arms sticking straight up. I was new at interpreting dreams. But my aunt Janice lived next door, and I knew she could help me.

I told my aunt Janis about the prophetic dream. I drew a picture of the dream on a big piece of paper to show her. It took up a whole page. I still have that drawing. One thing about prophetic dreams from God is they are clear. You rarely forget them. After listening to the dream, my aunt told me she had a friend who had a Bible study at the Pentagon in Washington.

She said that some of the ladies in her Bible study were also having warning dreams about something catastrophic happening on the East Coast. We continued to pray as the Lord led us.

When 9/11 happened, I knew I needed to go to New York and help in any way I could. I felt a strong draw to physically be there. I needed to feel and see the trauma. I had a desire to help the people and make a difference. This desire had to be from the Lord. I prayed and asked Him to open a door for me if He wanted me to go.

Not long after that prayer, a friend told me that a large church in the area was taking teams to New York City to minister. Each team would stay for a week. I signed up and was put on a team. It is hard to see and feel the reality of a crisis unless you are in it. I was about to be right in the middle of it.

I asked Jurgen if I could go. He said he would support me and help with our daughter, Heidi, while I was gone. I connected with my team at the airport. This was November 2001. The trauma and chaos were still in full swing.

There were about twelve people on my team. I knew no one except a friend from my church. We were happy to see each other. We stuck together like glue. Our team partnered with the Salvation Army. We stayed in an old Navy jailhouse and slept on bunk beds. The leaders knew it was a solid place to stay in case of another bombing.

When you volunteer in a crisis, sometimes you are taken to see the trauma. It is important for the volunteers to look at it and soak it in. This is necessary so the volunteers won't be distracted when helping others. The Salvation Army took us to the site where the towers fell. They gave us goggles, a hard hat, and a mask. We just stood there with our mouths open wide. I cannot even describe to you what that experience was like. We were now able to smell the smells and see the mangled metal and the destruction firsthand.

The Salvation Army gave our team three options in how we could minister:

1. We could help clean out the nearby apartments that were still standing. Many were full of ashes from the falling towers.
2. We could hand out stuffed animals to children who had lost a family member or a loved one.
3. We could go to ground zero (where the towers were) from 8 p.m. to 8 a.m. and serve the workers who were there to help clean up.

The workers consisted of construction workers, a cleanup crew, electricians, police, firefighters, etc. There were tents and tables set up with food, drinks, gloves, and hats.

Many of our team separated and did different jobs. My friend and I decided to minister in the tents at ground zero all night. We wanted to be with people, hear their stories, serve and pray with them.

The need was great in many ways. New York City is a small place. Most of the local people had a story of a loved one who had passed away in the towers. Almost everyone wanted to talk to us about it. Many people from all over came to New York City to help. We wore security tags around our necks. The local people would see the tags and thank us for coming and helping. They were grateful.

Our team served from sunrise to sundown at ground zero. We were right where we were supposed to be. We got the opportunity to give them hope and comfort. I know we picked the right place to be.

By the end of the week, we were able to minister, serve, and pray for over six hundred firefighters, police officers, construction workers, electricians, and more. We were full of the Holy Spirit, and His power kept us going. The people were wide open and appreciative. This was a window of opportunity to go into a place of trauma and make a difference. I am grateful we did.

My friend and I also got to go sightseeing. We went to the top of the Empire State Building to enjoy the view. We also rode on a double-decker bus and toured the city. I thank God for a husband who released me to go on this trip. He told me he was happy I finally came home because he had watched the movie *Bambi* with Heidi way too many times.

49

FIRST SPEAKING ENGAGEMENT

It was the year 2002, and we were growing quickly in the Lord. Our church was a big part of our life. There were about 600 people that attended. It has now been about seven years since I dedicated my life to the Lord. Every Christmas, our church has a women's Christmas event. It was a big event with food, beverages, worship, and a keynote speaker.

That year, the church asked me if I would be the keynote speaker and share my testimony. I was both delighted and scared. I never spoke in front of so many people. This was my church, and I knew these people. I was going to be vulnerable and share my story. I felt like I was ready and even excited about it.

I wanted to make a difference. I don't think it is a good idea to share your testimony too early. It is wise to get some healing before you open your past deep secrets too soon. I felt like it was the right time for me. I took it very seriously. I worked diligently on my speech. My cousin, Heidi, and her husband, Alan, helped me a lot. They helped me with the order of the speech and the integration of the scriptures. I spent many hours preparing. I was surprised by how much spiritual warfare was surrounding this speech.

I know now that I was taking ground back from the enemy. There is much power in our testimony. Everyone has a story. I know that is part of my purpose and calling. That is why I am writing this book.

2001 Keynote Speaker at Annual Women's Church Party

I dressed up for the women's Christmas party and was ready to go. I went into a private room before I spoke, and the Lord put fire to my mouth again, just like He had done when He healed me of stuttering.

I could feel His presence preparing me to speak for Him. It was a wonderful night as the Lord empowered me. I had the honor to pray for many people. They recorded my presentation. I duplicated that message and sent it to many of my friends and family.

I knew God was with me as I stood on stage and told the people all the wonderful things He had done. I knew and felt all of heaven backing me up. That night, I had a taste of what it felt like to walk with my purpose. God was redeeming the time.

50

REDEEMING MY WOMB

In 2004, I was feeling strange. I went to the doctor and found out that I was pregnant with our second daughter, Hannah. I was 41 at

the time. My girls, Heidi and Hannah, were five years apart. Words could not express how joyful we were as a family. In May, Hannah made a grand entrance into our lives and hearts. She came into the world saying, "Move over. Here I come!" Her sweet and loving personality made our lives brighter. Her funny and goofy humor made us laugh a ton.

Hannah had made our family complete. What a journey it has been to raise two girls. I have learned so much about life from being a parent. We spent a lot of time praying as we raised our girls. We had to rely on the Lord because I never felt well-equipped. The Lord helped us. He did not fail.

We put the girls in a Christian school for a godly foundation. In the later years, we put them in both public and home schools. After the birth of my second child, I was fearful about going back into post-partum depression. I hired a friend from my church to help me part-time at home. That way, I would get good help and rest. I never had depression again.

Baby Hannah

REDEEMING THE DANCE

My friend, Mary, who started the Wellspring Living Ministry, not only had a call to help women in trouble, but she also loved putting on large events. She helped put on a big event in 2004 with Beth Moore and Cece Winans. Beth was to speak and teach the Word of God. CeCe would lead worship.

This event was held at the 20,000-seat Philips Arena (now called State Farm Arena) in Atlanta in 2004. Mary found out it would be

Beth Moore's birthday on the day of the event. She wanted to surprise her.

Beth's favorite song was *Shackles* by the gospel singer duo Mary Mary. Mary had the idea that the girls in the Home of Redeeming Love would do a tactful choreographed dance to *Shackles* on stage for Beth Moore at the big event.

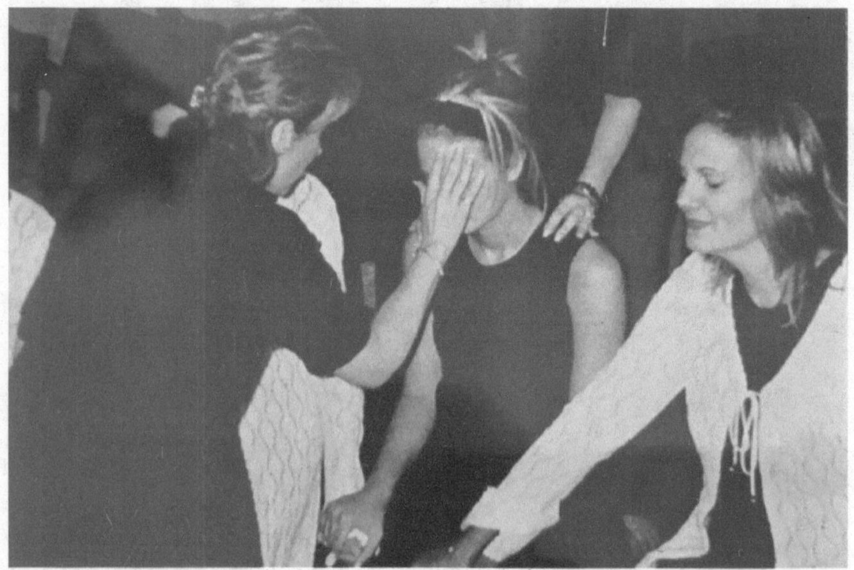

Praying for Beth Moore in 2004 at Philips Arena (State Farm Arena)

Mary knew that I had a gift for choreography. She asked me to teach the girls the dance. I was honored and terrified. I knew this would be a great way to redeem the dance. The enemy had taken my gift of dance, twisted it, and used it for his kingdom. Now, I would have the chance to worship the Lord on stage in a large arena with the girls in front of at least 20,000 women.

I gathered the girls to start practicing. We began working hard on the dance. The girls had come from different backgrounds. Some came out of jail for drug addiction. The others came out of the strip clubs or the sex industry.

Beth Moore and Attendees of Her 2004 Atlanta Event

I wanted the routine to be perfect. To be honest, I was frustrated because the girls did not have any rhythm. I went to the Lord and asked Him what to do. This is when He taught me the difference between perfectionism and excellence. He shared with me that if I did my best, taught the girls, and practiced hard, He would touch it, anoint it, and use it for His purposes. That was a great lesson for me.

The girls practiced hard in their spare time. It was all finally coming together. We went to Sears and bought classy outfits to wear for the performance. We purchased black pants, black shirts, and long white jackets.

It was finally time for our performance. On the day of the event, the atmosphere was charged with excitement. There were 20,000 women in the place. It was positively overwhelming. When we prayed together in our locker room before the show, Beth Moore came in to pray with us. It was a very holy moment that I will never forget. She poured out her heart to us about her past. We were all on our knees. She anointed us and prayed an individual blessing over each one of us.

It was finally time to perform. We were introduced by the MC. Beth Moore's band began to play *Shackles*. Surprisingly, the stage did not seem large enough for so many dancing people. It was a small miracle that no one fell off. We were right on cue and all together in sync.

The crowd got into it. They roared and danced and clapped. Some people were overcome with emotion and cried. God truly got the glory. He kissed the dance. Many testimonies came in afterward. I thank God that He heals and redeems.

In the years following the birth of Hannah, I focused on growing in the Lord, parenting, marriage, and ministry. I started my home prayer massage ministry. My friend from church would take Hannah while I had clients.

The Horseman Family (Heidi, 7, and Hannah, 2

I spent many years being trained by the Holy Spirit in what I call prophetic breakthrough prayer massage. It was the Lord's business. He would bring the people who needed a breakthrough or encouragement or just a place to rest.

I did massages from home for many years. It was a unique way for the Lord to touch His people. What an honor to partner with the Lord to birth ministries and to love God's people. For many years, I did this ministry in my home, in other people's homes, at spiritual retreats, and in other venues.

The more I ministered, the more I saw God's miracle-working power. It grew in frequency and intensity. Sometimes, the client would laugh with joy from heaven or just cry the whole time. Many people were baptized with the Holy Spirit on the massage table.

51

FEAR OF THE LORD

In 2007, I was upstairs in my home. I spent time worshipping the Lord. I cannot fully express what happened next. I believe I had an encounter with the Fear of the Lord. This is not a spirit of fear but the awe and reference fear of the Lord. The Scripture says, "The fear of the Lord is the beginning of knowledge, but fools despise wisdom and instruction" (Proverbs 1:7). The Fear of the Lord gives you humility and respect for God.

The remarkable thing about fearing God is that when you fear God, you fear nothing else. Whereas, if you do not fear God, you fear everything else. As I was having this encounter, I felt the atmosphere shift. I could not stand up any longer. I ended up in the fetal position.

My body shook because of the power of God's presence. I recall feeling small and being powerfully aware of His bigness. I knew that He could have taken me out right then and there. I was aware of my sinfulness and human weakness in comparison to His holiness and majesty.

I heard Him ask a question in my spirit. It was not an audible voice, yet I knew it was Him. He said, "Will you allow me to go big with your testimony?" I immediately said, "Yes, Lord, whatever you want." You can do whatever you want to do with my life. It is yours. My story is your story."

Very quickly, this encounter was over, and I was left there to ponder what had just happened. I thought it was kind of Him to ask permission for me to share my story. That encounter was a gift to me. It has been a wonderful reminder of how big God is.

Fast forward a few months. A new family came into town and to our church. They worked for Pat Robertson for CBN and the 700 Club. CBN stands for Christian Broadcasting Network. The 700 Club is a mix of Christian news and commentary and is well-known for its testimonies.

The guy who came to our church was named Sean. His job was to produce testimony videos for the 700 Club. He quickly heard about our testimony and wanted to talk to us about filming it to put it on the air. I remember the encounter I had with the Lord, and I knew it was Him who opened this door.

Sean did a video with both Jurgen and me together, which was too long for the show. Sean did a three-minute testimony with only me, and Pat Robertson accepted it. Pat Robertson was going out of town and did not want my testimony to be aired until he got home. He wanted to be the one to pray for people afterward. Sean did a great job with the video. Pat Robertson did a great job praying for people afterward.

The testimony was broadcast in October 2007. Jurgen and I had spread the word far and wide in preparation. Our church and family and friends watched. And according to the 700 Club, millions of other people watched that day. They said that many people called into the prayer hotline after my testimony to receive Christ. That made me happy.

It was prophesied to Jurgen and me that we have a media calling on our lives. I don't exactly know what that means, but we are willing to do whatever God desires to get the good news out. The media is definitely a good way to do that.

In 2010, I had the opportunity to meet with Janice VanCronkhite. She is known as a trailblazer in prophetic art. Janice and her husband lived in the Atlanta area and had a ministry to the poor named Blood and Fire. Janice heard about my prophetic breakthrough massage, and she wanted one. I saw her beautiful artwork and wanted to buy a few pieces. They were colorful and inspirational.

GOD'S CREATIVITY

At that time, Janice was painting at many different prophetic conferences across the country. She is well-known for her heavenly anointed, colorful paintings. She painted during the worship sessions. She shared with me her vision of having art retreats at her lake house on Lake Oconee.

One of Cindy's Paintings

The retreats began on Thursday evenings and ended on Sunday. Sunday morning was graduation. Everyone showed their paintings and shared what God had done for them on the retreat.

Janice named the retreats "Diamonds on the Lake." The reason for the name was because the reflection of the sun on the water resembled diamonds. She invited me to join her as an intercessor for the retreats. She also asked if I would give my breakthrough prophetic massages there. I was honored. Of course, I said, "Yes!"

The retreats consisted of anywhere between eight to twelve people. Janice did a lot of teaching and sharing of her testimony. She supplied the rooms and the food and fun. We had a time of jet skiing on the lake and resting. We also had prayer and worship time and plenty of time to paint and learn new skills.

Janice's desire was to help others reach their own imaginative pinnacle by tearing down the walls that kept them from pursuing their own artistic journey of heavenly creativity. She believed that art is an extension of God's creative love and His desire to speak prophetically to all people.

I partnered with Janice on many retreats. I was there to serve. I did this for about five or six years. I learned how to lead people and how to help them receive their spiritual and creative breakthroughs. I gave them tools to walk it out.

The retreats were supernatural. The presence of God was tangible at each one. This was an experience that made me grow in many ways. Many of the women who experienced the retreat took the impartation they had received back to their church or sphere of influence.

I asked the Holy Spirit to help me and teach me to paint. I was frustrated at first because I wanted to paint like Janice. It took time and patience. This was such an amazing time for me to learn to paint.

I now have forty paintings in my gallery. I have a Scripture on the back of each one. Janice was my teacher, and for a good while, I mimicked her style. But after a while, I learned to paint with more originality.

I sell my paintings at venues and give some away as gifts. People enjoy them because they have the presence of God on them. I am not an expert, but I enjoy painting with the Lord and playing with bright colors. I learned valuable lessons during this time. Most of all, God is creative, and He lives in me. So, I am creative, too!

LIFE COACHING

At the same time I was serving at the art retreat, I heard about a life coaching training course that was being offered in the area. It was led by my friend and mentor, Bonnie, and her son and daughter. They were passionate about helping others. They went to college to become certified trainers of coaches. They were zealous about it. They wrote a coach curriculum named *"Real Change Coach Training."* When I read that this training was for world changers and leaders, it got my attention.

They offered *Real Change Coach Training* to the community. The underlying meaning of their Real Change program was to help (R) restore, (E) equip, (A) activate, and (L) lead coaches. Their vision and passion were not just for individuals but to train and partner with corporate teams, universities, churches, and organizations. It was intimidating for me because it took a lot of studying and hard work. I had to bypass the lie that I was not smart enough and just take the plunge. I took the plunge and signed up.

This program gave me more tools to help people. I learned how to ask the right questions to help people get unstuck. I learned to motivate people to embrace growth, apply life-giving principles, and much more.

I am glad I followed through. It took me about a year and a half before I graduated. I received my Master Life Coach certificate in December 2012. It has not only helped me with my clients, but these tools have also helped me in everyday life with my family and friends.

SETTING UP MY MINISTRY ROOM

My training consisted of many tools that provided various ways to help people. I had been in the same church for almost twenty years. The church was in a large warehouse. I rented two rooms right outside the door that led to the church sanctuary. My pastor and leaders seemed to be fine with it. In the bigger room, I did my coaching, deliverance, inner healing, and art. My husband painted the room. It was beautiful.

We got a new rug and a nice big desk with two chairs. We framed a lot of my art and Janice's art and hung them on the walls. We put a small couch in the room, too. I also rented a smaller room beside that room. I used that room for my prophetic breakthrough massage. There was a bathroom right in the hallway, so it was perfect. I thought I would be planted there for a long time. Well, God had another idea.

MY FATHER PASSES

My father, at the time, had not been doing well. He had a stroke and then was diagnosed with Parkinson's. There had been a lot of healing between my father and me. I still struggled in some areas when it came to my family. I needed ministry. But not just any ministry. I needed wisdom, prayer, and guidance from someone experienced.

I heard about Pastor Olin, who was very experienced in deliverance ministry. He and his family had just moved into the area. I heard that Pastor Olin was very thorough and had a calling to be a spiritual father. I went to the little church he attended and approached him. He was with His wife and son. I told him that I had a call for deliverance ministry and that I would love to have a session with him. He and his family were very kind.

I went to my session with him and was impressed and happy that he was so skilled. He was like an experienced surgeon in the Spirit. I got a lot of help that day and was glad there was someone in the area like Him. I went home, and very shortly after that session, I got a call that my father was in hospice. I went immediately to say goodbye to my father and to pray for him to enter eternity.

NEW SPIRITUAL FATHER AND NEW ALIGNMENTS

After being there with my father for some time, I realized that what I used to struggle with concerning our relationship was not a problem for me any longer. Pastor Olin helped free me so I could be fully alive while saying goodbye to my father. After my father's death, I came home and knew that I needed to have the right spiritual covering and teaching for where God was leading us. The Lord told me to call Pastor Olin and ask if he would be my spiritual father and teach me what he knew.

Pastor Olin and his wife, Sherry, met with us many times. They agreed to become our pastors and teachers and our spiritual covering. Around that time, they started a church in their garage named "Agape Fellowship." We knew it would be a change of season for us. We were leaving the church that we loved so we could gain wisdom and skills in our special field of ministry. It was hard to say goodbye.

I describe it as a soldier going into boot camp. This is where you learn the basics of general warfare. Later, the soldier goes into more specialized training. For example, a sniper goes to sniper school. We had to leave our old church of basic training to enter our new church of specialized training. It was important for us to shift. We needed to learn much more.

NEW SEASON, NEW CHURCH

Agape Church was going strong. We were grateful to be starting on the ground floor from the beginning. Pastor Olin and Sherry were pioneers and had much wisdom, maturity, and experience.

Their spiritual father, mentor, and teacher was Henry Malone, author of the book *Shadow Boxing*. He is also known for his weekend freedom conferences. These conferences were deliverance and inner healing meetings that went on all weekend long. I attended some of these.

INVITATION TO LEAD A CONFERENCE IN TUCSON

In 2016, I got a call from Cindy, our pastor's wife, in Tucson. It had been twenty years since we had left Tucson. We had grown so much in the Lord since then. We were not the same people. Cindy was putting on a women's weekend conference at their church. She asked me to be the speaker. I was elated. Talk about a full-circle moment. Our whole family got to go.

Our church sent us out to Tucson with much prayer and support. It was a beautiful experience to go back and see the people who had loved us and never gave up on us. It was a big reunion and celebration. We also got to do a little sightseeing. My favorite thing was taking a helicopter ride over the Grand Canyon. It surely was grand. I was speechless with the awe of God.

CRISIS RESPONSE INTERNATIONAL

In 2017, a friend of mine from church asked me if I wanted to get trained with the organization *Crisis Response International,* or CRI. CRI is a Christ-based disaster response organization.

Training with Crisis Response International in Virginia

This ministry brings the light and hope of Christ to the darkest corners of the earth. Basically, CRI brings the gospel to the front line of disaster areas. They mobilize emergency relief supplies, volunteer workers, mobile kitchens, medical staff, chaplains, and more

I decided to go with my friend to the CRI camp in Virginia for their basic training. The camp was held at an old army training center. This was during the hot summer season. It was as hot as Hades. There were no comfortable beds or air conditioning. They explained that to train for disaster, you do not want to be comfortable. I enjoyed it because it took me out of my comfort zone. I learned a lot and met beautiful, like-minded people.

Soon after my friend and I completed basic training, we deployed together to Hurricane Florence. Hurricane Florence made landfall in 2018 at Wrightsville Beach, North Carolina, causing catastrophic flooding across the state. The devastation we saw was eye-opening and sad.

Our team split up. Some cleaned out homes that were flooded and beginning to mold. Others fed people from our mobile kitchen. There were also ministry teams and chaplains to comfort those who lost everything.

I went home and told Jurgen all about it. He wanted to be a part of this, as well. Jurgen took the basic training online. We heard about CRI putting on advanced training. Jurgen, my friend, and I wanted to go. The three of us flew back to Virginia in October to the camp. The weather now was so cold I almost froze. Again, we were not comfortable but grew much. We met more wonderful people. It was nice to have Jurgen with us this time.

After graduating from the advanced training summit, Jurgen and I went on our first deployment. We deployed with the CRI team to the terrible tornadoes in Alabama. The tornadoes were in Lee County. Twenty-three people were killed in the EF-4 tornadoes. The damage was incomprehensible.

Our team was able to get past the blocked-off areas because we were a disaster team. This gave us a huge opportunity to minister to traumatized people up close and personal. It was rewarding to make a difference. I enjoyed doing it together with Jurgen. We are better together.

Blessings During the 2020 Corona Virus Crisis

The year 2020 came with the crazy coronavirus shutdown. Our church banded together to pray and support one another. Surprisingly, we got a church building that same year. It was a nice building with lots of room and potential. In 2020, Jurgen and I and two other couples were ordained into ministry as elders of Agape Fellowship church. We were incredibly honored. *Look what the Lord has done!* He specializes in healing and redeeming.

52

BEGINNING OF A NEW SEASON

This is not the end of my story. It is the beginning of a new season and adventure with God. The acts of God continue in and through my life. My journey and walk with the Lord is not a sprint, but more like a marathon.

My purpose is to encourage and empower brokenhearted, hopeless, bound individuals to live a liberated, passionate, purposeful life by facilitating healing and wholeness and experiencing the love of the Heavenly Father.

I do this through the following ministries:

- Master Life Coach
- Deliverance and Inner Healing
- Breakthrough Prayer and Discipleship for Women
- Prophetic Inspirational Art
- Author of "Dancing with Deception"
- Inspirational Speaker

The Beginning...

THANK YOU

Many years ago, I felt the Lord wanted me to write this book. It was not the right time. My children were still young, and I had to grow and learn a few more things. We have a family friend named Eric Hill. He is a mighty man of God. He's the author of many books.

I called him and asked for his advice about writing my testimony book. To my surprise, He expressed interest in helping me. This book has taken me a year and a half to write. I could not have done this without him. I thank God for Eric's skills, patience, professionalism, and obedience to the Holy Spirit to follow through.

I also want to thank the people who supported me in writing my story. I want to thank my Pastors, Olin and Sherry Witherington, and Agape Church, for their love and prayers. I want to thank my husband, Jurgen, and my girls, Heidi and Hannah, for their patience and support. I want to thank Connie and Dave McBride and Sherry and Jeff Gossner for their consistent love and support.

As I finish up this book, I want to thank you for taking the time to read it. I hope you were touched by the incredible love of the heavenly Father. My prayer is that my story may give you hope and draw you to Jesus. Your past does not have to dictate your future. May God bless and keep you.

RESOURCES

- Contact me at Cindyhga@bellsouth.net.
- Wellspring Living: Program for victims of sexual exploitation; Wellspringliving.org
- Pathwaynetwork.net: "A life training sanctuary for women in recovery."

PRAYER FOR SALVATION

The most important relationship of your life is a personal relationship with Jesus Christ. If you would like to receive Him as your Lord and Savior and enter the greatest relationship you have ever known, please pray the prayer below:

Father,

You loved the world so much that You gave Your only begotten Son to die for our sins so that whoever believes in You will not perish but have eternal life.

Your Word says we are saved by grace through faith as a gift from You. There is nothing we can do to earn salvation.

I believe and confess with my mouth that Jesus Christ is Your Son, the Savior of the world. I believe He died on the cross for me and bore all my sins. He paid the price for them.

I believe in my heart that You raised Jesus from the dead and that He is alive today.

I am a sinner, and I am sorry for my sins. I ask You to forgive me. By faith, I receive Jesus Christ as my Lord and Savior. I believe I am saved and will spend eternity with you!

Thank You, Father. I am grateful! In Jesus's name, amen.